1 KINGS
Walter Brueggemann

KNOX PREACHING GUIDES
John H. Hayes, Editor

John Knox Press
ATLANTA

Library of Congress Cataloging in Publication Data

Brueggemann, Walter.
   1 Kings.

   (Knox preaching guides)
   Bibliography: p.
   1. Bible. O.T. Kings, 1st—Commentaries.
2. Bible. O.T. Kings, 1st—Homiletical use.
I. Title. II. Title: First Kings. III. Series.
BS1335.3.B789 1983   222'.5307   82-48093
ISBN 0-8042-3212-1

©copyright John Knox Press 1982
10 9 8 7 6 5 4 3 2 1
Printed in the United States of America
John Knox Press
Atlanta, Georgia 30365

Contents

1 KINGS

Introduction

The books of Kings are a passionate, intentional theological statement cast as historical narrative. Both the *statement* and the *casting* are important for preaching. Together they require the preacher to enter into the historical memory and crises of Israel to discern both the faith of Israel and the Gospel announced as judgment and as grace.

Introductory Matters

The books of Kings are comparatively simple, straightforward and well-ordered. So the critical questions are not terribly difficult.

(1) The *literature* of 1 and 2 Kings consists in materials drawn from many sources, now focused into a unity. The sources range all the way from official records of court and temple to popular tales of the prophets. The literature is now shaped around the interplay of three dominant positions.

(a) As the books of "Kings," the literature is structured to report in dispassionate ways *the sequence of kings* from David to the end of the political entity. This chronicle is stylized in the extreme so that the kings are summarized and assessed by a narrow range of criteria.

(b) But the more vital element, not necessarily expected in a chronicle of Kings, is the extensive *narrative about the prophets*. Compared to the chronicle of the Kings, the prophetic narratives are not so stereotyped or predictable, but announce surprise, intrusion and disruption, yielding on occasion either death or life.

(c) Closely allied with prophetic judgment is the regular attention given to the *function of torah* in the life of Israel, and the way torah is variously obeyed and disobeyed.

These three elements together announce what is structurally constitutive for the history of Israel. Anyone would readily assume that *kings* are constitutive, but this literature insists that alongside kings, *prophets and torah* are decisive agents of history. The narrative presents the interplay and tension of these three factors.

(2) At least on the surface, 1 and 2 Kings are *historical* narrative. That is, the text reports on the events and personalities that comprise the history of Israel (north and south) from 962, at the death of David, to 587 and the end of Jerusalem, together with a brief addition likely dated to 561.

Thus the text offers a considerable historical sweep, covering almost 400 years. But while it will be clear that this is a narrative account, our analysis will indicate that this is a surprising mode of historical reporting. It is not disinterested or objective in its summary, but is a narrative that argues a case and makes a statement.

(3) *The theological statement* over this long sweep is from the perspective of someone just before and after the debacle of 587. (Scholars dispute how much is from before the collapse.) In any case the literature as we have it is focused on that collapse, either in anticipation or in retrospect. Even the parts of the text that are rhetorically placed 400 years earlier (i.e., the Solomonic account) are now intended as a statement for the time and place of the collapse.

The events around 587 are understood as events worked out in the tensions among king, prophet and torah. The torah asserts the urgency of obedience, the kings variously honor and dishonor the torah, and the prophets anticipate the consequences of that obedience or disobedience. All of this together makes for an historical understanding very different from our modern modes.

Preaching Possibilities

It will not be easy to preach from the books of Kings. It will not be easy, first of all, because of our hang-ups about "objective" history. It will be difficult to make moves beyond the historical casting to the theological statement. That is, it is necessary to understand the nature and intent of the literature and to hear it in ways appropriate to its character.

But second, it will not be easy to preach here because the perspective of the narratives is abrasive and unaccommodating and not easily compatible with the culture embracing religion of much of the church.

My exposition has led to the conclusion that this literature which purports to *summarize* the kings in fact *delegitimates* the kings to show they have in fact forfeited their authority and are not really kings. Thus the book should be named with a question mark of incredulity—"Kings???"

Preaching might usefully address the following:

(1) *The ancient situation* itself can be usefully explored. The imagination of the church will be aided if we know the way our common past has been discerned.

(2) Our *present circumstance of politics* might be considered by way of analogy. Many important parallels come to mind. We must take care not to be reductionist, but there are illuminating points of contact, as we try to suggest.

(3) It is also possible, I submit, to teach these tensions in the text as *tensions faced by persons all through life*. This is a tension of *self-serving power* (read king) which always imagines it is autonomous, *a sense of urgent obligation* (read torah), and a *fresh wind which questions every old power claim* (read prophet). In some ways our lives are microcosmic scenarios of this same drama.

Preaching can be important both because material is given here which we do not know well and which regularly will surprise us, and because new categories for faithfulness are made available to us in these texts. Faithful preaching, I submit, is likely to be subversive, for this is a narrative about the painful, relentless dismantling of the known world.

The Dark, Ruthless Precariousness of Power: A Transition
(1 Kings 1:1—2:46)

These two chapters are commonly reckoned, not as the beginning of 1 Kings, but as the conclusion of the "Succession Narrative" (2 Sam 9–20). As literature they may be more properly attached to the book of 2 Samuel. In any case they function as a transition. They mark a literary transition into the books of Kings. Historically they mark a transition from one generation to the next in David's dynasty. In telling how Solomon became king after David, they struggle with the sordid manner in which power is lost and gained, transmitted and consolidated. The two chapters may be handled together in three stages. Together they show how *determined* is Solomon's grasp on the throne, yet how *precarious* is that grasp. The narrative can be the occasion for a meditation on the dangers, risks and demands of power and the seductive attractiveness of power.

(1) The principle of dynasty seems to have been established at David's death. But it is not clear which son can claim the throne now secure in the family. Two brothers, Adonijah and Solomon, both have notions of exaltation (1:1–53).

(a) Adonijah has a strong claim, both as the oldest living heir and by popular demand (vv. 5–10). But he is clearly at odds with powerful political forces which oppose him and support Solomon (see the hint in v. 10). So the issue is joined between brothers, but also between powerful and shrewd political factions.

(b) The Solomonic faction consists in shrewd and ruthless advisors: Nathan (the court prophet), Benaiah (an ambitious military bureaucrat), Zadok (a top clergy figure). Thus this faction includes the most knowing of prophetic, military and priestly leaders, and all this combined with the influential, intriguing queen mother Bathsheba. Notice how this triad of leaders dominates the story (vv. 10, 11, 32, 38, 44). Nathan is the brains of the plot, Zadok provides religious legitimacy and Benaiah is the ruthless hatchet man. Remarkably the Bible does not flinch from reporting on the charade of a strategy by which David the old man is deceived and exploited. A drama is staged with careful timing including the mother (vv. 15–20), the carefully planned entrance of Nathan (vv. 22–27) and the manipulated response of David (vv. 28–40). In order to understand this, the congregation might be led to consider contemporary political manipulations under Kissinger and the Viet Nam White House (e.g., *The Best and the Brightest*), the displacement of Cyrus Vance in the State Department because of Bzrezinski, or a myriad of other power plays.

(c) The result is a dramatic one (vv. 41–53). Right in the middle of their celebration, Adonijah and his supporters learn of the coup. They flee for their lives. The stakes are high. The others can flee. But Adonijah is too visible and public. He must make a public, humiliating show of subservience to the winners (v. 53). Thus in one quick chapter, a plot is implemented, an old man is duped, a favorite is outflanked, a throne is secured.

(2) The narrator interrupts the report of public events for a dramatic scene of death-bed instruction (2:1–12). David may be frail, but he has forgotten little, forgiven nothing. He is a ruthless man who has learned how to survive in the jungle. Survival is by killing all the dangerous ones before they kill you.

So after a proper and predictable allusion to Torah obedience (vv. 3–4), David gives advice concerning Joab (vv. 5–6), now of the hostile Adonijah group, Barzillai (v. 7, see 2 Sam 17:27–29, 19:31–40), a friendly chieftain whose support is valuable, and Shimei (vv. 8–9, cf. 2 Sam 16:5–14) who had earlier resisted and slandered David. The simple rule is to reward friends and destroy enemies, keep initiative at all costs in relation to all parties. The old man dies, having shared his cunning, bloody wisdom.

(3) Solomon is an obedient man (vv. 13–46). He listened carefully to his father. We are told about his callous, systematic elimination of all threats.

(a) The request of Adonijah (vv. 13–25) is an odd one,

sure to be perceived as rebellious and defiant. To ask for the concubines of the king is to ask for the kingdom (cf. v. 22, 2 Sam. 16:20–23). But it probably did not matter. On one count or another, Adonijah is too dangerous. He had to go.

(b) The others followed soon thereafter. Abiathar is banished, not killed (vv. 26–27). Perhaps as a priest he cannot be killed, because it violates his sacredness. Or perhaps he is not that dangerous. Solomon has a sure sense of where the threats are. Joab is obviously more dangerous. And so he is dealt with summarily (vv. 28–35). And that, even after his unswerving loyalty to David! But Joab guessed wrong on the succession. And he has only one chance. And Shimei is under house arrest. But in the end, he also must go (vv. 36–46). It may be ironic, or simply an oversight, that in vv. 5–8, instructions are given about Joab and Shimei (negatively) and about Barzillai (positively). But in the subsequent implementation, the positive counsel on Barzillai is absent. Has the new regime no memory for graciousness? Or at least a better memory for resentment than for kindness?

(4) This text will be an affront to many Christians. We will want to "spiritualize" it, or better yet, just skip it. So preaching from it will not be easy.

(a) First of all, it may suggest the real *flesh and blood* character of biblical faith. The persons in this narrative are real people with real agendas, with real shrewdness and real lust for power. And there is no other context for biblical faith. Thus the narrative permits a break with "Sunday School religion" which protects the Bible from reality. The future of God's people is worked only in the midst of such ignoble strategies.

(b) The narrative may suggest the fundamental contradiction of so much of human life, a contradiction seen by Paul (Rom 7:19–24) and so discerningly understood by Marx and Freud. David's charge in 2:1–9 evidences the contradiction so well, at the same time a charge to *ruthlessness* and to pious torah *obedience*. And that is the dilemma (here unresolved) of all persons who have *power* and seek to be *faithful*. How to be ruthless and obedient. This text provides no way *out*, but at least it is a candid way *into* that dilemma. And sometimes preaching should not lead people out of, but into reality.

(c) In terms of biblical history, these unflinching chapters help us to see the shaky and ambiguous foundation of the Solomonic throne. Solomonic texts (especially when selectively handled as they are in the church) may show him to be gracious, faithful, wise, noble, etc., etc. But power has its darkness. And the Bible honors that darkness from the beginning. Power is based on the capacity to compete in ruthless ways for dubious prizes. If the Bible is anything, it is knowing about power. (That this candor is a heavy awkwardness is evident in the expurgated version of 1 Chron 28–29, in which the succession is uncontested and positive. There is no more conflict and no more counsel to vengeance. The realities of life have been "cleared up" for the sake of blind faith.)

(d) In a less direct way, this narrative retells the model narrative of Gen 3–11. This dispute among brothers sounds like a restatement of Cain and Abel which can only end in murder. And it echoes the yearning of powerful ones to make their own name (Gen 11:4, see 1 Kgs 1:37, 47). Thus the Bible understands this particular encounter to be yet another embodiment of the "human predicament" of power grounded always in ambiguous and contradictory packages.

(e) Should the preacher wish to risk it, this narrative provides opportunity to raise the question of darkly seized power in every area of life. How have things gotten arranged as they have and then been legitimated? How is power, influence, food, money arranged in the family, in the congregation, in the world of nations? It is the case that every legitimated form of power has underneath it something less noble, more likely to be ruthless, exploitative and self-serving. This narrative permits those who want to, to probe the uneasy darkness, to discover why we sleep so restlessly on the heap of power. For we all play many roles in the drama of power: the cunning Bathsheba, the bloodthirsty Benaiah, the vulnerable Adonijah, the uneasy Solomon who cannot sleep until it is settled. And our communal life insists on our moving in and out of these roles. The text invites us to a realism about ourselves. Thus the narrative may open new attention to public forms of power. But it may also open to us the darker realities which beset us all the day, and more ominously haunt us through the long night.

The text finally offers no resolution. Its ending is terse:

"So the kingdom was established in the hand of Solomon" (v. 46). But that does not end the story. It only begins the rule of ambiguity and precariousness. Such a way to power never leaves one safe. There was a hint of "a more excellent way" in 2:2–4. But it is scarcely noticed and not at all heeded in the rush to self-securing.

The Solomonic Evidence
(1 Kings 3:1—11:43)

The first major block of material in the books of Kings is 1 Kings 3–11, a report on Solomon. This material is presented as an historical narrative. But it clearly has been shaped as it is to function as a theological statement.

(1) Like much of the books of Kings, this material makes use of and relies upon a great diversity of *older materials*. This includes temple archives (with special reference to the building of the temple), royal records, liturgic fragments and popular tales. But it is clear that this is no longer presented as a straight, primary reportive literature. It is now intended to serve as secondary, reflective material in order to make a theological point. It operates with some reflective distance from the events it characterizes. In many instances the preacher will be able to discern the tension between the flat, factual presentation and a deep, theological discernment.

(2) The *theological power* of the material is handled in two ways. First, there are noticeable *insertions of self-conscious theological materials* at some points. Second, there are careful *placement and location of materials which are older* but are now used in self conscious ways. A sense of theological coherence is provided, especially by the "envelope" of chapter 3 and chapter 11. A second device which is important is the juxtaposition of the two dreams of chapter 3 and chapter 9. A third such effort is the placement of chapter 8 at the center of the report to focus on Solomon as the faithful temple builder.

(3) The following exposition suggests that this material partakes in *a keen sense of irony*. That is, the literature seems to say one thing, but for those who are perceptive, something else is also asserted beneath the surface of the literature. That is, the narrative subtly calls attention to the incongruity between what appears to be true and what is in fact going on. And that incongruity is a useful homiletical entry into the text. The statement of incongruity is understated and not blatant, as though the narrator is aware of the ambiguity in rendering such judgment.

But in the end,

> The wise king is in fact a fool about things important.
> The king who loves Yahweh in fact loves "many foreign women" who subvert his faith.
> The king who seems to embody prosperity and well-being in the end offers only oppression.
> The king who sets out to obey the torah ends under harsh prophetic judgment.
> The temple built as an act of obedience becomes an entrapment for God.

(4) The entire piece is a part of the larger statement of Deuteronomic history. All of it together evidences that Judah as well as Israel is *on its way to judgment and destruction.* The narrative considered here carefully hints, but does not say too much. And that is not because it does not know, but rather it is an artistic achievement that *discloses but does not reduce* the inscrutability of the historical process. This narrator knows about the shape and main claims of the historical process. But at the same time the story is told to allow for freedom in that process. And the preacher will take care to do the same thing.

Out of all this comes an awareness that the narrative is not much interested in the person of Solomon. In contrast to the literature on David, Solomon does not seem to have fascinated Israel. This literature focuses not on the person of the king, but on the claims and possibilities of the historical process which God finally will govern. Preaching from this material requires us to let those claims and possibilities be recognized again in our own experience of God's governance of history.

A Rightly Based Beginning (3:1–28)

After the ruthless coup of chapters 1–2, this chapter portrays the beginnings of Solomon's long rule. Preaching here might raise the question of how faith makes a beginning at living. What foundations are essential for the beginning of faithful living, for the beginning of a new season, indeed for the beginning of a new day?

(1) The note in vv. 1–2 is *a warning of realism.* Faith has always to live in a context. The context of Solomon is the

world of international politics. Solomon all his life long was preoccupied with Egyptian power. It is clear that Egypt was not only a contextual presence, not only a potential ally, but also a constant seduction. Solomon imitated much that was Egyptian. We know he modeled his government after that of Pharaoh. Here we are told he made an alliance. And finally we shall see in chapter 11 that these kinds of alliances and marriages contributed to his downfall. Clearly he also adopted social practices and social policy from a regime that was incongruent with the dreams of justice and freedom which are definitional for Israel.

Preaching here might ask for a realistic assessment of our context for faith, the ways in which the context may support, the ways we make alliances that may be supportive and costly, the ways in which we imitate and are seduced. Our contexts are never neutral, but they may, without our knowing, talk us out of our faith. A sermon here might easily raise the complex questions of faith and culture and the ways in which the faithful are regularly compromised, often unwittingly.

(2) But the context of vv. 1–2 only prepares the way for the foundational story of vv. 3–15. The story is well-known, and for good reason. It presents Solomon as a model of faith, his life and his rule so far uncomplicated and uncontaminated by the ways of unlimited power. The text suggests a paradigm in which the young king is not preoccupied with Egyptian alternatives. For this instant he is preoccupied with faithful, obedient prayer.

(a) A sermon might approach the practice of prayer both with evangelical affirmation and with critical awareness. Good rule and good living begin in prayer. But it is not just any old prayer. It is prayer which submits to God's will, which is not preoccupied with self, which does not use "address to God" as a way of self-serving. Solomon's prayer is one without guile, indeed "like a little child." The prayer is from one who has no claim to make, who "empties himself" and is prepared for obedience. The prayer waits on God without ready-made answers about the use of power.

(b) The prayer does not begin with petition. There is not first of all asking, but *remembering* (v. 6). In the prayer Solomon sets himself in the history of Yahweh with his people.

The context for prayer is a recital of the long history of graciousness which reshapes and redefines this moment of prayer. Such prayer is never in a vacuum, but always in a context of faithful remembering and a grateful resolve to continue this family in faith.

(c) The petition, when it finally comes (vv. 7, 9) is not for self. Hans Walter Wolff has observed that this prayer is a contrast to our modern propensity. The king asks not for self, but for the capacity to do his work better. He asks for a "listening heart," that he may not be beguiled by administrative procedure, that he may not be constricted by what is on the surface, but that he may discern what the human dimensions of reality are. Solomon's prayer is linked to his vocation of rule. He does not ask for personal gain, but for the good rendering of his call. Such prayer concerns the embrace of one's vocation, and very likely faithful prayer is always linked to one's call from God.

(d) The gospel in this narrative is that God's gifts go well beyond royal asking (vv. 10–13). For starters, Solomon is given what he asks. He is given a heart to do well. But beyond that he is given precisely what he did not ask—riches and honor even beyond Egyptian patterns of wealth. The miracle of this prayer is not only that God answered the prayer, but that the answer utterly outdistanced the request (see Eph 3:20). The assurance is not that God answers prayer, but that the answer completely surpasses the request. All because "your heavenly father knows you need all these things."

(e) But note (in v. 14)—perhaps added, perhaps not—there is a provision that all the gifts are linked to obedience. The narrative is undecided on this question. But it is not an indecision of weak resolve. It is an unsure decision because life is precisely like that. God's gift is indeed utterly free and at the same time, God's free gift beyond our asking always carries a mandate with it. The dual nature of God's way with us is not because of unresolved theology, but because of the mystery that belongs to every serious, gracious relationship. So at the very moment of assurance and affirmation, the king receives a sobering warning. When God's way is disregarded, everything is in jeopardy. And as Solomon was to learn, there is no amount of self-securing which can circumvent that footnote.

(f) The prayer encounter was a dream (v. 15). Of course it was. Prayers consist in dreams beyond present reality. Dreams are times for new resolves, for fresh configurations of reality. And here at least, Solomon is a child of the dream. He is ready to embrace the new ways of being king. He offers thanks for the new beginning bestowed on him. And he gives a feast for his servants. The new gifts from God are translated here into gifts for the people. ("The gifts of God for the people of God.") It is a show of *generosity* which does not yet anticipate the *exploitation* to come. For now Solomon is willing to have his life shaped by a dream which at least temporarily shakes him out of the stereotypes of oriental tyranny. The dream and the prayer permit "a new creation," even in the context of Egyptian imperial seductions.

(3) Solomon's dealing with the two women (vv. 16–28) is perhaps the best known tale about the king. The story itself is a common tale which occurs in variant forms in many cultures. So we do not know whether the story is factual. But that does not matter. The story is placed where it is to model the ways of the king, who has just been entrusted with a hearing heart.

(a) The story is set in vv. 16–22. The story lacks all specificity which suggests it is intended to serve as a model for how a wise king characteristically rules. The narrative concerns not the concrete, but the typical.

(b) The Solomonic part in vv. 23–27 is dominated by the speech of the king:

Then the king said (v. 23),
And the king said (v. 24),
And the king said (v. 25),
Then the king answered and said (v. 27).

This is now Solomon's world. He proceeds with skill and clarity. There is no uncertainty on his part.

(c) The verdict of v. 28 is what counts. The narrative serves the reputation of the king. Israel sees the rule of Solomon as a rendering of *justice*, but even more as a show of *wisdom* from God. The story serves to legitimate Solomon as one endowed by God. The promises just made by God about wisdom are kept. The prayers of the king are answered.

Perhaps the story can make its own way in preaching. But I would be inclined to handle the text with Niebuhrian irony. What in fact does the story mean to tell us? No one can doubt that the decision is likely correct. Or that the decision is likely reached in the only sure way it could have been. But what is missing here is any show of compassion, any human dimension, any indication that the king cared very much. A sermon might make the hard point that the use of public power cannot be reduced to romanticism and that public officials cannot personalize decisions the way "religionists" might like. The sermon might help a congregation think about the gift and the danger of public power, about cold objectivity as a stern form of compassion, about the practice of justice being very close to cold cynicism.

But as this management of wisdom portrays no compassion or romanticism, it also gives no hint of vengeance. Nothing is done to the woman who ostensibly lied. She is not punished or condemned, only sent home without the child which was not hers.

There is no doubt some irony in the narrative. And as we shall see, Solomon's wisdom in the long run turned out to be foolishness. But for now, wisdom makes its careful way between a *compassion* that would be maudlin and a *vengeance* that would be destructive. That kind of distance for seeing clearly and without complicatedness must be a gift from God. In a society where the hairs of justice are infinitely split, perhaps it suggests that the community of faith has a stake in letting justice in the public domain be nine parts simplicity and common sense. In such a court as this, even the poor and disadvantaged have a chance.

What's an Imperial Court Doing in Israel?
(4:1–19)

It is unlikely one will preach on this text. But if one has the patience (both the preacher and the congregation) the text suggests some knowing possibilities. The marvel may be that this text is here at all. For it reflects a well-developed bureaucracy which seeks to reduce everything to a manageable system. Solomon clearly believes that the "system is the solution." Effort is made to comprehend everything, to administer all the goodies and to outflank all the unresolved aspects of public reality. This text gives one pause as to how such an enterprise could be legitimated in Israel which began as a community of liberation which withdraws from Pharaoh's Egypt. And now Solomon has reintroduced Egyptian models into Israel. With good reason, George Mendenhall calls this the "Canaanization of Israel." Specific elements in the bureacratic inventory might be noted:

(a) The main officials in vv. 1–6 likely are the same ones who intervened on his behalf at David's death. There are no "new faces" in Washington this year. It is the same crowd that has a sure instinct for survival and for power. And when the same names regularly recur, one may be sure that an elite is emerging which knows first how to cover its own flanks and serve its own interests.

(b) Note especially in v. 6 that there is a "secretary for labor." And that is "forced" labor. The sad tale of Solomon in chapters 11–12 is that his whole house of cards collapses under the weight of conscripted labor for state projects. But here the department is legitimate and unembarrassed, right alongside the priests. It makes one wonder how "kept" the priests were, to sanction and agree to such exploitative enterprise. Did the priests not notice? With what were they too busy?

(c) The long list in vv. 7–17 is clearly for taxation. It is a tax collecting network to produce vast sums of money for the central government. One may be sure that the tax network was exploitative and that the ill-defended were exploited the most. And one may be equally sure that the system served to enhance the inequities, that the "establishment" lived on the produce of vulnerable citizens. Now of course such a criticism is not spelled out in the text. But there is no doubt that such a system served to institutionalize injustice in the name of "peace and prosperity."

(d) It is commonly agreed that the entire system of organization, efficient as it is, is taken over from an Egyptian model. The names of the offices indicate that. A preacher might well play on the presence of such a "military-scientific-industrial complex" right in the midst of this community committed to freedom and justice. Such an incongruity in the text might help us look more unflinchingly at the comparable incongruity in our own society.

The point is that this is not an innocent, neutral list. It is rather a heavy commentary on the path to destruction that this regime has taken. How incredibly far the actual practice of Solomon has come from the innocent prayer of chapter 3!

Preaching on this text will in any case be provocative if not risky, if the text is seen to be more than a telephone directory.

(1) The congregation should be amazed that such a list is in the Bible, a list which smacks of oppression, of institutional exploitation, which believes anything is legitimate if it is done in the name of the system.

(2) One might faithfully preach a sermon which would initially give comfort to the enemies of big government. The text means to suggest that such a vast network surely breeds exploitation and leads to trouble. So a sermon might have as its theme "get the government off our backs."

(3) But one cannot stop there. If one stops there the sermon might comfort the wrong folks and in any case miss the point. For the point of the list is to serve the inordinate affluence of the well-off and especially to enhance a strong defense budget. That's what most of the revenue went for and still goes for. Therefore this sermon should comfort no one, not the ones who want to reduce government, not the ones who want a big defense budget, not the ones who believe the government can solve all problems. But the critique is not made on the grounds of political insight. It is based rather on the need for justice and wisdom which comes out of Solomon's dream and Israel's memory. And that tradition harshly judges every systemic reduction of reality.

(4) If these entries are too heavy, then the text might address persons who need to reduce all of their personal lives to a system of order in which everything is accounted for. That is, the political shrewdness of the text can also make a psychological comment about the need to try to tame, reduce, domesticate and administer every aspect of our lives. That will not work. Because there is passion and there is terror. And if they are not given room, they will break out in other ways more deathly. The final question is not political. It is rather the certitude we have that life, public or personal, can never be reduced to a system. There are wild dimensions to life which even Solomon's management experts could not get

their hands on. Failure to allow for this administrative wilderness in life is a dangerous foolishness.

A Program and a Promise (4:20–28)

Solomon is an embodiment of efficiency and prosperity. He offers an opportunity for reflection on our own efficiency and prosperity. The present text surely celebrates the accomplishments of Solomon. But it also offers a subtle critique of those same achievements. So a sermon might develop which both *celebrates* and *criticizes* contemporary modes of well-being.

There is no doubt that Solomon was able to create a most remarkable economic situation, one of "peace and prosperity." Israel puzzled over that fact, and with some ambiguity. On the one hand, anyone who is that successful must be blessed by God. On the other hand, Israel knows that Solomon is not only not a *pious* man. He is not a *compassionate* man. It appears that much of his achievement depends on a *cunning and ruthlessness*. Those marks do not easily go along with blessing from God. So the issue about which Israel is uncertain is this: is Solomon a bearer of God's blessing for his people? Or is Solomon a betrayer of Israel's deepest dreams? The evidence is mixed. And articulation of that mixed evidence may be the task of the preacher. Our own "peace and prosperity," such as it is, is equally ambiguous. It is a gift from God, but perhaps also a work of cunning and ruthlessness which betrays our deepest dreams. Clearly, Israel was boggled and bothered by Solomon, not knowing what to make of him. And not knowing what to make of him, we scarcely know what to make of our own power and well-being, our peace and prosperity which in part is based on cunning and ruthlessness, in part a gift from God.

(1) The text opens in vv. 20–21 with a sweeping statement. It summarizes the issues.

(a) V. 20 offers an ideal of unmitigated well-being, abundance overflowing. The "sand of the sea" indicates that now the oldest promises and deepest hopes of Israel have come to fruition (Gen 22:17; 32:12). It is indeed a miracle to celebrate. (On the miracle of multiplication, see Deut 10:22.) The phrase, "eat, drink, rejoice," bespeaks God's full approval (see Eccles 9:7), and a profound temptation (Luke 12:19). Referring Solomon's enterprise to Luke 12:19–20, one may wonder if they were "rich toward God." And one may ask, "And the things you have prepared, whose will they be?"

(b) V. 21 suggests the economic basis for this well-being. Solomon stands at the center of an empire, shrewd, and undoubtedly ruthless and exploitative.

(c) The remainder of the program is reported in vv. 26–28. It indicates extensive military arms (v. 26) which are never lightly supported but depend on heavy taxation. It also describes a network of tax agents (vv. 26–28) whose purpose is to deliver what the king needs to satisfy his bureaucratic appetite.

The picture of the whole is an oppressive, self-serving regime. Some surely did "eat and drink and rejoice." But others (non-Israelites and undoubtedly Israelites) ate much less, drank what was left over and rejoiced only occasionally (cf. Luke 16:19–31). What impresses one is the cynical summary which simply disregards the inevitable social counterparts of such a regime. The program is a facade of general well-being, and the narrative does not willingly permit us to see behind that appearance. That appearance may be a reality. More likely it is a cover-up.

(2) Except for v. 25! I suggest this verse is the preachable point in the text. It is odd here, out of place. It is not a part of the royal program. This single verse appeals to the old covenant promise of Lev 26:5 about "dwelling in security." And it claims the visionary anticipation of Mic 4:4. This verse of safe, serene vines and fig trees is Israel's oldest image of well-being. Note the contrast of the luxury of vv. 22–23 and the modest hopes of v. 25. Here there are no consumption-oriented values, but only a modest, intimate hope, not for abundance, but for enough. This promise is for enough, but not more.

In order to help folks reflect on our own public values of a consumptive kind, it will be well to note the incongruity between the Solomonic *programs* of vv. 22–24, 26–28 and the old *promise* of v. 25. The intent of the text is that the program will fulfill the hopes of the promise.

But it cannot! And that is the point. The *program* is a fundamental contradiction to the *promise*. The promise envisions a social order in which there is stability based on equity so that none has designs on the modest stake of the others. And the reason one person can rest content with his/her vine or fig tree is that it is certain that the neighbor is also content with his/hers and has no designs on this one. This is not a romantic agrarian vision but a realistic note about ordering public life in ways that are not rapacious. And the way to so order public life is to end arms races, to terminate vast public expenditures for defense. That's the promise and the condition of the promise (see Mic 4:3 on disarmament as a prerequisite for this vision of social reality). The primary threat to one's vine and fig tree is not anarchy, but a state controlled budget which must have more and more to sustain itself. And in the end, the state apparatus consumes the very thing it claims to protect (see Hos 7:9).

Solomon's *program* is just the opposite of the *promise*. It is a vast, self-serving enterprise which operates by force and depends on an enormous tax system. And the tax system to support such domestic extravagance and such arms is aimed precisely at modest claims to fig trees and vines. That is, it must tax away the very thing it promises to preserve. The narrative, I suggest, operates at three levels:

(a) It is at first glance *an historical report*. It describes what is happening.

(b) It is *propaganda*. It makes the best possible case for the regime, arguing that the program of the regime will give the promise; i.e., arms, taxation and usurpation will give secure vines and fig trees "with none to make afraid."

(c) But finally, I submit, the text is *ironic*. That is, its real intent is something other than first impression indicates. It wants us to recognize that v. 25 cannot be comfortable with vv. 24, 26–28. The program cannot keep the promise. The program denies and contradicts the very promise it claims to give. So what has happened? The deep promise of ancient Israel has been confiscated as ideology for the state. The very promise it depends on is defeated by its grasping style. Hope has become ideology.

The sermon which might be preached here is to help the church think about the contradictions between our programs and our promises. Our present system (in church and in society as well as our personal ways) cannot keep the promises

we most treasure. Indeed, our systems of economics and
politics which manipulate and coerce, deny our hopes. And
we are left with the rhetoric of our promises but no substance beyond the conjured needs of the corporate
consciousness.

The preacher can go as boldly as he/she will. The promise in the simplicity of Mic 4:4 can be reasserted. That is
what we yearn for and what is promised. But when that
promise is clear, it will also be clear as well that the program
of false needs and consequences erodes the promise. The
preaching task here may be to put folks in crisis, or to help
folks make sense of the crisis we are in. And the conclusion to
be drawn? Perhaps that if we really cherish the promise of
well-being, "with none to make us afraid," the program of
arms, consumption and taxation must be dismantled. The
text purports to speak of the enhancement of the sytem. But
there moves here an awareness of the dismantling to which
Israel is called. And that dismantling is now at issue, a dismantling that must take place in the public domain, but perhaps first in the imagination of the citizenry. In Solomon's
Israel, the dismantling gathers momentum in 1 Kgs 11–12, in
the surprise of the prophets (1 Kgs 11:29) and the hostility of
the labor force (11:28, 12:1–4).

Wisdom Which Is Sheer Folly (4:29–34)

Solomon has a secure reputation for wisdom. But the
biblical narrative account suggests he may have been wise
on the short run, foolish for the long stretch, wise in small
things, foolish about large matters. This brief account by itself is uncritically affirmative about Solomon's wisdom.

But even there, the wisdom attributed to Solomon pulls
in two directions which do not easily cohere. On the one
hand, wisdom has its *source* in God (v. 29). The characterization of this verse is compatible with the gifts of wise rule giv-
en by God in 3:3–14 (cf. 2 Sam 14:17). But on the other hand
and in tension with that is the *use* of wisdom reported here.
In vv. 30–34, we may suggest that the skill and erudition de-
scribed concerns an enlightened, exceedingly pragmatic and
calculating regime.

(a) The measure of wisdom in vv. 30–34 is "the other nations." Solomon invariably keeps an eye on this comparison,

for he is determined to be like the other nations—only more so. Such wisdom is not characteristically Israelite, but is rather a move away from Israel's identity as the people of Yahweh.

(b) Gerhard von Rad has argued that this kind of wisdom is an inventory to organize, classify and administer learning. That is, such a churning out of "summary statements" in the form of proverbs concerns not simply artistic imagination, but the organization of knowledge for use. It seems probable that this wisdom is not for the love of learning or for appreciation of life's mystery, but that it is at the brink of usable technology. Now that is not bad, except that it affirms that wisdom then becomes not an end, but a means. Knowledge is valuable as it is useful for other purposes of the regime. Such a view fits what we know elsewhere of Solomon. Wisdom like everything else he touched has become a commodity.

(c) In v. 34, it is suggested that all this learning is not a joy in which to delight, but a device for another purpose, namely, beating the other nations at their own exotic games. This verse anticipates the visit of the queen of Sheba in chapter 10.

I suggest a sermon on this text might move in two directions:

(1) One might consider the tension between the *source* of wisdom and the *use* of wisdom. In v. 29, the source is clearly God, the one who grants insight from the throne of majesty. In vv. 30–34, the use is surely to master and impress the nations. Such a *source* and such a *use* do not fit together easily. Is such a use a betrayal of the source? And from this one might reflect on the use of gifts in general, but specifically on the purpose of science and the temptation to technology, the acquisition of knowledge and the strange ways in which knowledge serves power. On the slippage *from source to use*, one might consider 1 Cor 13, a meditation on the function of knowledge and the alternative of the gospel. In such a technologically fascinated culture as ours, one might ask about the prospects of our much "wisdom."

(2) Or one might face the large question: what is it that constitutes *true wisdom*? One might ask about Solomon's wisdom which used people, indulged self and ended in disarray. Is there a wisdom which discerns and acts faithfully?

And how is that related to our modern modes of knowing and controlling? Moves to the NT should not be made easily. But it is clear that Jesus is perceived as a bearer of wisdom (see Mark 6:2), indeed a child of wisdom (Luke 7:35). Or conversely, one may turn from Solomonic wisdom to the Pauline notion that human wisdom is criticized and broken by the cross. What a dangerous judgment that: "the foolishness of God is wiser than men" (1 Cor 1:25)! The cross is indeed a scandal to every wise person (1:33). But the contrast between Solomon and Paul on wisdom should not be an excuse for obscurantism. It rather affirms an opportunity to celebrate human capacity to rule as "the image of God," and yet to consider that all our wisdom becomes a charade of self-interest. In the end, the wisdom of Solomon is not different from the wisdom of the king of Assyria who refers to "*my* wisdom" (Isa 10:13). When wisdom becomes autonomous as *my* tool and *my* instrument without reference to God who authorizes and governs it, wisdom becomes not only a *self-deception* but a way of *self-destruction* as well. There is a "shame" awaiting all those who imagine too much from their own wisdom (Jer 8:8–12).

Sure Temple/Precarious Torah (5:1—7:51)

Solomon is supremely the temple-builder. He is predestined to fulfill that function (cf. 2 Sam 7:13, reiterated in 1 Kgs 5:5). The narrator, utilizing detailed records, takes a long time to report the whole enterprise. Obviously the temple is crucial to the story and to the entire history of Israel. This extended account of the building is not very well ordered. And we cannot review it here in detail. It will suffice that we should comment on some items in the narrative.

(1) The building of the temple needs to be understood in terms of Israel's changed social circumstance. While Israel was concerned with survival, a temple was a luxury not to be contemplated. It is only when Israel comes to security, abundance and prosperity that temple building comes to mind (5:4–5, see 2 Sam 7:1–3). Thus the temple may be a religious act. But it is also an act of social and political solidarity to give expression to a broader social achievement. That is, the temple is a political statement as well as a religious gesture. The temple expresses a view of reality concerned for *stability*.

Its symbolic function is to focus, assure and authorize social stability. The temple corresponds to a *royal view of reality* which always impinges upon and dampens God's terrible, terrifying freedom. That is, we are now confronted with a religion of stability, no longer a community of critical protest. That may be a point worth noting in church contexts with an "edifice complex."

(2) It is now clear that the temple (unlike the ancient "Tent of Meeting": see Exod 33:7–11) is a foreign architecture in Israel, reflecting a foreign theology, an alien notion of God's presence. It is not unimportant that the key workmen are Phoenician (7:13–17). There is some confusion in the name Hiram, used for both the king and the workmen. Note the distinction in 2 Chron 2:11–14. But that is unimportant. A careful review of temple symbolism indicates the points of tension here with Israel's faith:

(a) The symbolism is *cosmic*, in contrast to Israel's covenantal tradition which is primarily historical and specific.

(b) The room arrangement, with special reference to the "inner sanctuary" (6:23), reflects *a notion of divine presence* at variance with Israel's memory. On the one hand, the several rooms make a *hierarchal* distinction. The people are clearly second-class participants in relation to the elite who have access. On the other hand, the Holy of Holies suggests an *abiding* presence, in contrast to a God who comes and "meets" (Exod 33:7–11), but who comes and goes and does not "live-in." On both counts, the danger and surprise of Yahweh's presence in Israel is reduced. God is now domesticated. And one must weight the *gain of guarantee* against the *cost of perversion*.

In that context, one may consider the threat to the temple posed by the "death of the king" (see Matt 27:51). This is not to say the temple is not "biblical," but that it lives in a harsh tension with other biblical traditions. The temple is not socially disinterested. Understanding the temple and our attraction to it requires that we attend to the vested interests which cluster around it.

(3) The temple building was a great public works project. While the leading artisans may have been foreigners, the lackey work was done by citizens, and not all willingly (5:13). Thus there is an *inescapable linkage between the temple (to the*

glory of God) and forced labor (to the oppression of neighbor). It is at least ironic if not blatant criticism, that this symbol for God's sure *presence* should be the occasion for social *oppression*. But that is what it is.

It is conceded in 9:23 that Solomon had a great public works program. In 9:22 it is claimed that the project excluded citizens and used only non-Israelites. But 5:13 seems to make the case differently. And in any case, we know in 11:28, 12:1–14, that forced labor and state policies of coercion were the cause of the kingdom's disruption. Temples are not socially neutral. They tend to embody the religion of the "dominant class." That is, they are characteristically committed to *order* at the expense of *justice*.

(4) The temple is closely linked to the Solomonic construction of the royal city. That is, the temple seems to have been one necessary (but only one) building in the royal complex. The temple is like a church in a suburban development. You must have one, because it contributes to the coherence and stability of the whole. While the temple took seven years to complete, the palace adjacent took thirteen years, suggesting it was even more elaborate and more important (6:38—7:1). While biblical theologians might want to make more of the temple religiously, we here may see it as a part of a grander political scheme to enhance Solomon. And if that is the case, it is beyond doubt that the temple's function as *guarantor* rather than *critic* is foremost. It is likely that in its main function (by design as well as practice), the temple was not a gathering place for the people, but a royal chapel. Like its royal counterpart in the north (Amos 7:13), this is a place where transcendent, critical principles are not likely to have their say.

(5) Probably not too much should be made of a single item. But as illustrative of the problem, we may focus on *cedar* as the material of the temple (5:10). Cedar had to be a foreign import and therefore also an expensive commodity available only for the very rich. The homes and churches of the poor are not panelled. In some ways "cedar" may be a code word for such inequitable wealth. Reference could be made especially to Jer 22:13–17 in which the prophet juxtaposes cedar/vermillion with justice/righteousness. Clearly the one cannot be traded for the other, even though Solomon

tries to do it. The temple of *cedar* can never be far removed from *forced labor*. For there surely cannot be such an inequitable distribution of precious wood without such exploitation.

Now I am aware that I have presented a critical, perhaps negative view of the temple, likely reflective of the Protestant penchant of the expositor. That may be an overstatement of the text. And the preacher will want to make his/her own judgment. At the very least what is offered here may be a good test case for interpretive principles, to show that different interpretative principles, applied to the same text, can yield very different expositions.

The justification for this tendency in exposition is found in the character of the literature. What is before us in the text is not a report on temple building. Rather it is *a report on temple building* used in order to comment on *the disarray in Israel's history*. The text asks how temple-building is related to historical disarray. Thus I should argue that in its present form, the text presents an essentially protesting, critical view of the temple. The narrator does not want to detract from the greatness of the Solomonic achievement. But the theologian is unambiguous that "temple" is no adequate or ultimate principle for social life. That adequate and ultimate principle is found only in the *Torah*. And the temple must be subsumed under, held accountable to, and judged by Torah. Thus there are likely several sermons here under the general rubric of *temple and torah*. Temple here represents every attempt to consolidate, stabilize and make secure. Torah, by contrast, is the principle of protest and precariousness which lives by the risk of obedience. Temple and torah are always in some tension. And that tension is not just an ancient problem, but one transposed into our own situation.

(1) The clue to this juxtaposition is perhaps found in 6:11–13. Here the theologian does not appeal to ancient record but uses his own formula. And he reverts to his standard phrasing of "if . . . then" (see 9:1–9) which premises everything on obedience and makes everything conditional. Clearly the temple is no adequate principle, nor an alternative to torah obedience. The well-being and effectiveness of the temple depend on the "if" of "walk in my statutes and obey my ordinances and keep all my commandments and walk in

them." Temple is made marginal to torah religion, even with all these verses of extravagant description.

(2) If this entire literature is written as a reflection on exile (as we presume), then there is *realism* in this critical view of the temple. For in anticipation of 587, or in reflection upon it, it is clear that the temple did not and could not save Israel. It is no enduring principle, for the Babylonians can destroy it and God can depart from this house. What this historian knew and what the exiles discovered, is that when all is lost, one cannot return to "old time" Jerusalem. But one however can revert to obedience to the torah. It is torah which characterizes Israel, not temple (Deut 4:5-8). And in the tough times coming to the American Church, torah and not temple will be our mode of well-being and faithfulness.

(3) This theologian is a close associate of Jeremiah, in tradition, even if not in chronology. There are of course various traditions about temple in the OT, and this is not the only one. But I suggest a special kinship between this casting of temple and the great polemical statement of Jer 7:1-15. Again it is clear that torah and not temple matters.

(4) Jesus' disputes with the religious leaders of his time focused in part on the temple. Both his radical assertion of Lordship (Mark 11:1-19) and his enigmatic threats to the temple (John 2:13-22) reject the ultimacy of the temple. Indeed in the NT it is the *person of Jesus* (the new torah) which displaces the temple.

Kings must build temples. In the long run, Solomon would not have been a king without a temple. But temples are always penultimate and never final. In preaching from these materials, the preacher will need to locate the symbolic equivalent of temple for his/her congregation. The issue turns not on "attachment to a church building" but on any attempt to locate in life a safe place where God is guaranteed and where we are immune from the stresses and demands of historical life. Such a "free ride" may be found in something religious, such as piety, dogma, morality. But it may also be found in an ideology of economics, politics, psychology or whatever. This text suggests on the one hand a penultimate value of and care for such safe places. But on the other hand it warns against imagining such constructs are ultimately safe, for the holy danger and freedom of God will not be domesticated. Finally, the Son of Man, the Lord of the temple (and of the entire community of faith), has "nowhere to lay his head" (Matt 8:20). Solomon resisted that truth. But Israel learned it again and again. Thus the tension of temple and torah is a discernment of a key task of every human life, of wanting things secure and yet having things always as provisional as God's call to new obedience.

The Battle for God's Presence (8:1–30)

The desire to have God present in our midst is a perennial one. It is a yearning for blessing and order and well-being. Sometimes Israel regards God's presence as precarious, unsure if it can be counted on (see Exod 33:15). At other times, Israel boldly claims God's presence as if it is a right upon which to presume (Exod 17:7, Jer 8:19).

In what ways God is present in Israel is an old question (by the time of Solomon) and clearly disputed. On the one hand, the old tradition regarded God's presence as a danger and Israel keeps some distance (Exod 20:18–20). At other times, the presence of God is quite concrete and identifiable, even material (Num 10:35–36). These various tensions and alternative postures come to full expression around the question of temple-building (2 Sam 7:1–7). Israel knows that the temple is a problem because it seeks to *guarantee God's presence* but it also *presumes upon God's presence*. And one is left with the wonderment. Can God's presence be guaranteed without presuming upon it? And that issue is not simply an old, traditional question. It is exceedingly contemporary, even if we articulate it differently. One cannot live for very long with precariousness as the main mark of what is holy. Yet we also know that the holiness of God, when it is reduced to safety, loses its power to give life.

This text is a pivotal one for Solomon. Before it, Solomon is the faithful king with much *promise*. After this chapter (immediately in 9:1–9), a new sense of *threat* is introduced. So here is focused a great deal of what Israel believes not only about the temple but about the prospect for a king who must have God present and who seems to violate God's freedom in the process.

But the text is more than a statement about Solomon and his temple. It is a battleground among Israel's theologians for a faithful understanding of God's presence. The chapter is a complicated one which developed over a long period of time. And during that time, different voices in Israel have their say. The battle over God's presence is never completed but always needs to be faced again. And it is a struggle not confined to Solomon's time. For there are evidences of skirmishes in the text both early and late in Israel.

(A) The text contains at least three opinions about God's presence with the people, all serious alternatives in tension with each other. Part of the job of interpretation is to show that there is no single answer which is "right," but different proposals are placed alongside each other.

(1) The first and most obvious affirmation is given in the elaborate ceremony of vv. 1–13, culminating in the poem of vv. 12–13. Here presence is connected with the ark (see Num 10:35–36). In old and uncritical materials, the public presence of God is identifiable in liturgical fixtures, furniture and actions. This is the most public and popular notion of God's presence. It is also fairly naive, for it does not see any danger, problem or complexity related to the matter. It takes religion for granted and believes that good religious practice lets us live at some ease with God's real presence (see Amos 6:1). It is, of course, essential to manage the process carefully, and that is the business of knowing priests. When such care is taken, it works!

(a) Special attention should be given to vv. 12–13. These are commonly thought to be very old, perhaps from the time of Solomon. They are a doxology which celebrates God's public presence. God *sits* (dwells) in Jerusalem. He is not going to leave but has settled in. And it is *forever*. The royal apparatus has allied itself with God. There is no threat, but only a benign transcendence which gives easy legitimacy and assurance. Such a notion precludes any idea that God might stand over against the social order in any effective way. God is friendly and readily accessible to sanction what is underway.

(b) The priestly theology of Solomon (see vv. 10–11) draws upon the high liturgical tradition reflected in Exod 24:15–18, 40:34–38. Both the term "cloud" as well as "glory" here offer a static, reliable notion of God's in-dwelling.

This theology has an important social function, even if

uncritical. It gives legitimacy to the public order. It authenticates and authorizes institutional structures and supplies the cohesion needed for communal life. It provides a "sacred canopy" (see Isa 4:5–6) over the regime and the community without which life is not possible. It gives a symbolic barrier against the threat of jungle existence. For good or ill, this is an ancient equivalent of civil religion. And there are important times in life, e.g., at death, when the assurance of such a reliable God is an important pastoral act.

(2) The assertions of vv. 27–30 reflect second thoughts. They are likely from another time and place and from persons who do not accept the uncritical assurances of vv. 12–13. These verses do not affirm the static presence of God who is always available as the primary temple theology affirmed. Here is offered a much more awesome view of God, one who transcends every human construct, intellectual and visible. It knows about the mystery of God who will not be boxed in or domesticated. It understands that God has kept to himself (in heaven) the mystery of his person. God is not fully placed at the disposal of earth, nor of the managers of religion. This God is not a friendly partner of the cultural establishment, but an awesome lord, distant but attentive. I judge this a much more refined theological statement, for only such an awesome God, free from all our constructs, is a help beyond our ingenuity. Only a God free from us can finally help us.

Thus the linkage made by this text is the daring affirmation that *the free God* (v. 27) is *the God who helps* (vv. 28–29). This theology is not against the temple. It still values the temple as a special place for approach to God. But it holds more modest claims for the temple. Now God's person is free from the temple, but God's *eyes*, God's *ears* are turned to Jerusalem. He has accommodated himself to special human needs. Note the evangelical difference. The God of vv. 10–13 is not a God who acts or intervenes. He abides but does not do anything. And the people who practice such religion do not have needs, but only say doxologies.

But this God (in vv. 27–30) acts. And the worshipers have needs. They know something is wrong which they cannot correct. Thus the theme of *presence* is translated to *forgiveness*. This is not a God at our disposal, but one inclined in gracious ways who makes a difference. With this God, there is a chance, even though we know how we really are. It is not more than a chance, but it is the only chance. And now faith is not an assurance of God's visible *presence*, but a trust in God's *inclination* toward us. This theology cuts underneath civil religion to genuine evangelical confidence. It touches more elemental human agendas and so lives in some tension with the rather simple-minded religion of the royal regime. In moving through this text, the congregation can move from a *surface* religion to a genuinely *pastoral* religion. Because what is yearned for is not simply a God who *upholds* the order, but one who intervenes with forgiveness to *restore an order* now lost among us.

(3) The move from vv. 12–13 to vv. 27–30 is a move from *surface* to *pastoral* theology. Now we may note a second move, made rather discretely in v. 9. In the midst of all the buoyant pageantry of Solomon's process, some puckish theologian has added a note of acute criticism. In a ceremony which assures that God is fully present, this verse is a bucket of cold water dashed upon all easy assumptions and too easy religion. It is as if to say, "Oh come on, now really!" God is not that easy for us. And in fact, this whole religious enterprise has not captured God. The ark is empty. The throne is vacant. God is not here. This is not atheism, but the sober affirmation that God stands free from our best efforts to confine him. So we have not simply a pastoral theology which assures forgiveness, as in vv. 27–30. Here in v. 9, there is a move from *pastoral* to *critical* theology. This critical theology stands against every cozy and surface religion which knows too much and presumes upon God.

Even the festal procession must advance in God's *absence*. The *faithful presence of God* is here characterized as *God's sovereign absence*. But the text does not leave the ark finally empty. In the ark are the tablets of the torah. The tablets are not a substitute for God. But they are what is given to us to honor, trust in and rally round in the face of God's freedom. Israel, according to this theology, is not permitted to draw too close (see Exod 19:21–25). In this narrative, Israel's mode of God's presence is the practice of obedience. That is, the cultic agenda of worship is transformed into an ethical agenda. *Attention to God* is transformed into *passion for the world*. Obedience is not an afterthought, but it is Israel's way of being with God. So John Calvin could write, "All right knowledge of God is born of obedience" (*Institutes* I 6. 2). Thus v. 9 is an exceedingly bold note, daring to raise torah-obedience as an alternative mode of knowing God, alternative to conventional religion.

(B) A sermon on this text can help the congregation with the difficult issue of God's presence. People are often misled by thoughtless or manipulative religion. Here is a chance to help people through the problem of God's presence in which a great deal is at stake. It will be helpful if the question of God's presence is *linked to Jesus*.

(1) There were already in the NT unthinking, conventional religious notions about Jesus. This is indicated in the response of Peter in the transfiguration narrative. Peter misunderstood and wanted to build booths so that he could "contain" Jesus (Mark 9:15). The same misunderstanding is evident in the cynical argument of the disciples concerning power in the coming kingdom (Mark 10:35–37). Both on the mount of transfiguration and on the way to Jerusalem, the disciples misunderstood. And they wanted to reduce Jesus to easy, power-bestowing religion.

(2) That *surface* religion misunderstands. It is called into question in Jesus' peculiar attention to and care for the marginal, the ones who stand most in need of forgiveness. Thus the forgiveness theme of 1 Kgs 8:27–30 can be linked to Jesus. The radical *pastoral presence of Jesus* is evident in Luke 7:36–50. Jesus announces the deepness and danger of forgiveness which is not available to those who live conventional lives, short of compassion. This narrative shows that Jesus makes the move from conventional to pastoral faith.

(3) And the second move (see 1 Kgs 8:9) from *pastoral* to *critical* faith is made by Jesus when he announces that he must die. That is, his presence is only as "the Crucified One," the one who declares every other religious notion as empty and void of power as is the ark. Jesus announces his call to obedient death. This in turn is linked to radical obedience for his followers in the call to discipleship (see Mark 8:34–36, 10:21). Thus the presence of Jesus is known only in the practice of obedience unto death. And where such obedience is not practiced, Jesus' presence will not be known. *Presence* is

redefined in terms of *crucifixion*. This means the end of every
conventional way in religion and in society. His subversive
teaching about presence culminates in John 2:19–21, where
he speaks of the temple to be destroyed, which (we are told)
is a reference to his own crucifixion and resurrection.

In these moves, I suggest, the issue of God's presence is
presented in a Christological way. The preacher has opportunity to see that the question of presence touches our deepest
assumptions and perceptions about reality. Everything is
transformed by the way of this free God who is present, but
who may also absent himself from our best efforts at
containment.

Exiled, Cared For, Summoned (8:31–65)

1 Kings 8 is a long chapter into which many persons and
groups have introduced their notions about the temple and
the presence of God. We have suggested that in vv. 1–30 we
may identify at least three competing opinions about God's
presence in the temple. The remainder of the chapter, vv.
31–65, is a series of later derivations which reflect even more
developed notions about God's presence. While it will be difficult to do in a sermon, the most interesting preaching likely
will be to show that these opinions are all there, that they
exist in some tension with each other, and that these various
opinions continue to be operative among us.

(1) The theologians of Israel recognized that the temple
theology of vv. 12–13 claimed too much for the temple. That
is a very "high church" notion of God's physical presence.
They did not want to affirm that, but wanted at the same
time to claim access to the mercies of God. So in vv. 31–45,
there is a stylized narrative which catalogues the troubles
which may come upon Israel—defeat, drought, famine, pes-
tilence, war. The narrative affirms that all troubles are to be
referred to this God of all mercies. That is the main teaching
here, and in fact it has little to do with the temple as such. So
an evangelical sermon can be preached asserting that this
God is indeed responsive to the need and hurt of Israel. Trouble is to be taken to the Lord in prayer. But that prayer is not
linked to a place. It is linked only to faithfulness.

(a) The main petition is that God will "hear in heaven."
The prayer may be offered in the temple, in this house, at this

altar. But the text is not overly committed to temple practice. The temple at most is a place wherein people can turn to the transcendent God who dwells in splendor beyond all our architecture and formulations. But the news is that *God hears*. God's people in trouble are not alone. There is a God who hears and we are the people who both bear witness to that and practice it. The text forces the community of faith to decide about our modernity, about "death of God," about our secular competence. And it insists that such deep needs must be referred to the Holy One. And it affirms that there is one who hears.

(b) But the hearing is accompanied in each case by a more profound affirmation, that *God forgives*. The entire recital of trouble is portrayed as a result of disobedience to God. Thus the troubles of life are discerned in terms of guilt and forgiveness. They are understood in intensely theonomous ways. There is no part of life which is not referred to God. And there is no part of life that lies beyond God's graciousness.

(2) In vv. 46–53, the prayer continues with a more specific reference. Now the exile of Israel is anticipated. But the formula is unchanged. Again it is a petition that *God will hear* and an anticipation that *God will forgive*. Exile is, among other things, a sense of remoteness from God. This is a bold prayer which affirms that there is no remoteness from God which God cannot penetrate. The evangelical point scored is that our remoteness from God is overcome by God's will for nearness.

(a) In v. 50, the double use of "compassion" asks not only that God should have compassion, but that their captors (the Babylonians) should be compassionate as well. This is indeed a prayer that asks God's will be done on earth as it is in heaven. The confidence of the prayer is that God can move not only to be directly gracious but that God will work in ways that change social relationships.

(b) But Israel dare not pray for forgiveness or hearing or compassion without also remembering who Israel is to be (vv. 51–53). Israel is the people peculiarly chosen and treasured by God (see Deut 32:8–9, 11), the "apple of his eye." Israel is God's special inheritance, desired by God and set apart for God's purposes.

A sermon on this text might talk about both *the grace*
and *the call* of God. The grace of God is that our troubled
lives never drive us far from God's nearness. But the grace of
God is given precisely to a community of faith which knows
its identity and understands its purpose in the world. The
mission is never removed from the grace, but the grace is
linked always to the mission.

(3) The narrative announces the graciousness of God. But
in vv. 54–61, there is a kind of realism about God's expectations and mandates. In the preceding verses, there was expressed a great hope for compassion. But here the text
returns to the main claims of Mosaic faith. The primary way
to know God is to obey God's commandments. The structure
of this unit is characteristic in Israel. There is first an announcement of God's fidelity and promise-keeping (vv.
56–57). But this is immediately followed by commandments
in a way that echoes the claims of Deuteronomy. Preaching
from this unit will not be terribly innovative. Because the
main issues before God's people do not require a new thing
be said. They require rather to say the old, reliable thing
with freshness. And here it is clear and simple. To be Israel
means to *rely on God's promises* to the exclusion of every
other reliance. To be Israel means to *keep God's
commandments*.

The other curious thing to observe here is that in v. 59, it
is as though Solomon's intercession continues to have effica-
cy for the times to come. It is his prayer to be near God all
the time, that God may establish the cause of Israel. A sermon here might reflect on the power of intercession, on the
urgency of leadership that turns the need of the people always to God. And most of all it may lead to a recognition that
what we most yearn for is that our cause should be established, i.e., that we should be treated equitably.

(4) This long history of temple theology reaches its conclusion in 8:62–65 with a great festival. The feast is extravagant, too big for the altar (v. 64). This episode portrays the
delight of Israel who is utterly blessed, completely reassured,
opened to lead a "new and righteous life." The foundation for
life is now settled in gratitude, in joy and in gladness for
God's goodness. Even this impressive Solomon is presented
here as one who receives good gifts, who relies not upon what

he can conjure, but upon the blessing of God, richly and free-
ly given.

The temple is a sign of the redefinition of all of life. Israel
in this scene affirms that life is an *utter gift* from God. And
this gift requires a *full response* of grateful obedience. Such a
text leaves us with a lot of hard work. How ought *gratitude* to
be enacted? What shape ought *obedience* to take? The text
leaves that much still to be decided.

The God Who Speaks Twice (9:1–9; cf. 3:5–14)

Sometimes a good sermon emerges from letting two
texts rub together so that each of them comes to mean
something it did not mean alone. Texts get changed by the
company they keep. An instance of this might be the inter-
relation of 1 Kgs 3:5–14 and 9:1–9. The first of these is likely a text from Solomon's time. That is, it might be a report
of an actual event. The king very well might have begun his
rule with a ceremonial journey to Gibeon. That showy inau-
gural culminates in a dream which brings a word from God
which reshapes the monarchy. So the formula issued: "At
Gibeon the Lord appeared to Solomon in a dream by night.
And God said. . . ." Solomon's reign begins in a word from
God.

There is no need to be distracted by the notion of a word
in a *dream*. It either happened that way, or it is a stylized
device to introduce a weighty theological point. We cannot
tell which. Either way, it is an assertion that Solomon is not
on his own. He is not autonomous, but the initiative for his
life and rule belongs to God. It is God who speaks. Solomon's
task is to listen and answer.

In contrast to this early and likely genuine positive
word, the narrative of 9:1–9 is a very different thing. The
formula is different: "The Lord appeared to Solomon a second time, as he had appeared to him at Gibeon. And the Lord
said to him. . ." (vv. 2–3). The narrative clearly looks back to
the dream of chapter 3. It could be that the two dreams are
both narrative reports of what happened. More likely, the
second is an intentional fabrication which imitates the first
dream. The second one concerns much more intentional and
heavy theology. The word of the "second time" is like a theological clarification or corrective of a point that was not orig-

inally clear. It is like a second thought on God's part (see Gen 22:15). The development of a sermon from these texts might include the following:

(1) We do not live by what we can make on our own. We live by the inscrutable surprises that come to us. Here the inscrutable surprise is a word from God which comes in the form of a dream. The word of God is concrete, exceedingly difficult to define, but most important to biblical faith and to the current practice of faith. It is not a hallucination, not necessarily the hearing of voices. It is, rather, a deep certitude of being addressed, claimed, named, taken seriously and caught by an overriding purpose. The notion of "word of God" is terribly deceptive because we easily identify our own imagination with the word of God, and so we hear God echoing back to us what we wished to hear in the first place. Except—we may be very sure that the second word here is not an echo of anything Solomon wished to hear.

This text is beyond our usual self-deception. Neither the historian nor the king doubts that this is a genuine word from the Holy One. The word from God is always concrete, so that it redefines our situation in life. It reminds us that we are not our own, but we belong to another who comes first to us. One of the important agendas for any person who would live powerfully is to discern what is God's word to us which redefines our life. Here the word of Solomon is that even this powerful king is *not free* to use his power as he chooses. Even he must answer to the hopes of this other one who is really God. That is, God's word requires the king to recognize that God is God and that king belongs to God. That becomes clear because this God speaks yet a second time, beyond the conventions of the first time.

(2) The word from God to Solomon offers two kinds of messages. The first word God speaks (in the first dream) is a word of *permission* and *gift* (3:3–14). So we might ask, as Solomon had to ask, what do we really want for our life? What are we to do and what do we need to do it? The word from God in 3:5 is an invitation to ask (see Matt 7:7–12). The word announces that God is a generous Giver. The dream makes clear that what is needed for life is granted as gift. And what a gift! A discerning mind (vv. 9, 12), riches and honor (v. 13). This text for this terribly calculating king affirms that "all

good gifts are sent from heaven above." There is something playful in this text, inviting us to think through: What one thing would we ask from God? And what other gifts might God give that would surprise us? We can ask something of God. Solomon's request is so remarkable because it is an *obedient asking*. That is, it is congruent with what God wants to give. And it is consistent with who Solomon is called to be. His asking is appropriate to the proper relation of God and Solomon. So his is a faithful, obedient asking.

But the gift is a part of a larger process. What happens through this dream exchange is that Solomon is legitimated as king. That is, God gives Solomon *permission* to live as a powerful king. Solomon here knows what we are so long in discovering, that we cannot easily or comfortably live unauthorized, "unpermitted" lives. Such a way of living leaves us restless and malcontent. So there is in Solomon's prayer all the mystery of freedom and predestination. Solomon is the perfectly free man. But his legitimacy from God ordains and destines him to be the king he intends not to be. Archbishop William Temple observed that real joy occurs when what *we want to do* with our lives is identical with what *we must do*. God's word is an empowering permit to us. And only with the permit can we live genuinely free lives, not self-invented. That's a gift.

(3) But there is a second word which comes to us in 9:1–9. It also is a saving word from God. But now it is a word of threat and warning, a call to accountability, an awareness that if God's call to us be mocked, there will be a sorry result.

The text is symmetrical:

v. 4 if . . . . v. 5 then,
v. 6 if . . . . v. 7 then.

The first pair speak about *obedience and well-being*. The second pair talk about *disobedience and humiliation and judgment*. It is a tightly arranged pattern in which life is reduced to a neat formula.

That's a tough word out of which to preach the gospel. There is too much tough religion that is only social control. So the threat may be only our mothers' biases, or our guilty consciences, or peer pressure or calloused morality. From whence comes the threat in our lives? And too many sermons have frightened, wearied or scolded people on doubtful grounds. Any sermon on this text must avoid such cheap manipulation.

But finally this second dream is not about superficial moralism or coercion. It is about the awesome, dangerous claim God makes on his creatures. Solomon was a man of enormous power. And in our best human power, we are tempted to "outgrow" obedience and do things "our own way." The word is precisely for celebrated humanity "come of age," tempted to imagine that God is a fading hypothesis now to be discarded. Such human pretense tends to relativize all of life, to imagine that every norm is only a convenience to be sloughed off. This text draws a line against every prideful moralizing to assert—even against the mighty Solomon—that God's intent of an accountable humanity endures in the face of every human ambition. God finally is not mocked. Life has moral coherence and the measure of life is found in the torah, in the concrete guidance, reverence and accountability at the center of life.

This second dream makes an almost awkward claim. It announces that even in the majesty of downtown Jerusalem, the old boundaries about killing and coveting, about sabbath and neighbor, still are the key to life with God in God's world. Nothing has changed that.

(4) The possibility for a sermon is that *both words* from *both dreams* must be heard. And mature faithfulness is in living in tension between the two words, not being able to escape the tension nor to choose either word over against the other. The two words of God are not just alternative human inclinations. Rather, they are the ways in which God's sovereignty is shown to us. And we must take account of God in both his postures toward us.

Obvious Glory/Hidden Anxiety (9:10—10:29)

These verses are a rather miscellaneous collection of information. They provide a general characterization of Solomon's reign and are placed rather casually between the theologically intentional statements of 9:1–9 and 11:1–13. Together with 3:16—4:34, they tell us most of what we know about Solomon, apart from the temple. Since the text itself is a series of brief, disconnected notes, we may comment in the same brief, disconnected fashion.

(1) Solomon has engaged in a political and economic treaty with Hiram, King of Tyre (9:10–14). Solomon's specific gain was material and scientific "know-how" for building the temple (5:8–12, 7:13–14). Solomon was to give Hiram in return produce (wheat and oil, 5:11). And now we are told he also ceded to him twenty cities. The incident suggests that Solomon was a wheeler-dealer on a very large scale. It may also suggest he was a trader with a very sharp pencil. Perhaps he bested Hiram in these exchanges. Probably the story has its origin in the aetiology of "Cabul." That is, the story served to explain the name and origin of Cabul (9:13). In any case, Solomon is here something other than a pious temple-builder.

(2) "Forced labor" is definitional to Solomon's regime (9:15–23). And that requires an extensive bureaucracy to bring it off (see 4:1–19). Forced labor was necessary to achieve the grandiose schemes of the regime, to imitate and surpass the royal pretensions of comparable regimes. Specifically, the forced labor was for armaments and storehouses, i.e., items military and economic. The qualifying statement of v. 22 excluding Israel may or may not be correct. But in any case the policy indicates how completely the Exodus tradition of liberation has been perverted if not nullified. The whole enterprise is premised on inequality sustained by harsh coercion. One might observe the incongruity of temple-building and shabby economics. But more likely temple religion supplied a necessary legitimation for such exploitative economics. It was because of that same economic oppression that Solomon's reign came to a sad end (1 Kgs 11—12). Worship of false gods (11:4–5) carries with it exploitative social policy. Such social policy and such religious ambition go together. Together they constitute a policy of "being like the other nations" (1 Sam 8:5, 20). And this community cannot be like the other nations *in temple-building* without inevitably being like the other nations *in social practice*.

(3) Solomon could make it big in the world of international competition (9:24–28). It is all of a piece. His replication of foreign rule includes:
(a) alliance by marriage (v. 24; see 9:16, 11:1–2),
(b) pious public (exhibitionist?) religion which ensured legitimation but hinted at no practice of self-criticism (v. 25), and

(c) commercial trade, so that Solomon is the broker for much of Near Eastern consumerism (vv. 26–28). Alliances, religion and trade all work together. The preachable point here may be the way in which religion becomes a comfortable, accepted part of an exploitative regime. This religion is completely enmeshed in the system and has no critical distance from the system. Clearly for Solomon, *"the system* is the solution," not the torah nor the God of the torah.

(4) Only one narrative is offered in this array of summary texts (10:1–10). And because it is an extended narrative in a collection of "notes," more detailed attention may be given to it.

King Solomon is of course noted for his wisdom (see 1 Kgs 3:16–28, 4:29–34, 5:12, Prov 10:1, 25:1). The wisdom of Solomon provides an issue for a sermon concerned with human knowledge, human technology and the apparent capacity to sustain and transform our modern world. The text permits an exploration of the possibility and limits, the risks and opportunities of human imagination.

(a) At the outset, it will be necessary to understand Solomon's wisdom in its own context. "Solomonic wisdom" does not refer to a personal gift or virtue of the king. Rather, it more likely reflects a cultural phenomenon and a structural achievement which Solomon was able to initiate and which he shrewdly administered.

The wisdom for which he is famous is likely an imitation of and borrowing from the imperial ways of the great powers, especially Egypt. That is, Solomon seeks to be "like the other nations" (see 1 Sam 8:5, 20), to emulate their abilities in terms of administrative finesse, economic and political savvy, cultural sophistication and religious urbaneness. As Solomon replaced the other powers, it is likely that he was drawn further away from the specifically Israelite-covenantal understandings of reality. Thus the very wisdom celebrated constitutes something of a threat to the faith of Israel. The very wisdom celebrated is perhaps a *development* of Israel's faith, but it is also an *assault* on it.

The interpretative move which can be made is to raise a question about American wisdom=ingenuity and technology. Such "wisdom" may be a development in the service of our best values. But it may also be an assault on those very values. There is little doubt that Solomon's wisdom caused his regime to forget the Lord of freedom and justice (cf. the exodus) and to think it had wrought all those wonders by its own power. And the question may be raised if the same move toward cultural-religious autonomy is not visible in the successful "wise" American consciousness.

It is most probable that the wisdom of Solomon, so much celebrated, is not disinterested. That is, it is utilitarian, to serve the other ends of the government. Thus wisdom (technology, technical know-how) is used to produce wealth, to raise the standard of living, to mobilize resources, programs and persons for the goals of the state. The very wisdom seen in Solomon is treated critically in the stories of Joseph and Daniel (Gen 41:8, 15–16, Daniel 4:6–18) as the cynical capacity for power in other kingdoms. The Bible is not unambiguously positive about this kind of wisdom (see the extreme form in Isa 10:12–13).

A sermon might be offered from this text which pursues the links to our own cultural sophistication, high standard of living, affluent economics and capacity to mobilize knowledge to serve the interests of the governing groups. In both ancient and modern times, the same wisdom which is a *gift* from God is a *threat*. For it tempts us to imagine autonomy, to assume that our ability rather than God's goodness is the source of well-being (Deut 8:17). Solomon is at the brink of such fatigued autonomy. A preachable point is that we are also near the brink of thinking that, because of such power through knowledge, we are free to devise whatever goals we like. The purpose of such a sermon might be to help people explore the deep ambiguity of our modern capacity, to see the very ability we celebrate as a temptation which can lead to destruction. Our text mostly celebrates. But I would suggest hints at a more discerning understanding of the matter.

(b) The dramatic power of the narrative consists in the *queen's surprise* at Solomon's well-being, and the *queen's response* to what she sees. Obviously, what she encounters is beyond her expectation.

(i) The visit of the queen is ostensibly to check out Solomon's wisdom, i.e., to find out if he is as good as his reputation. But it is more plausible that the meeting is an example of personal diplomacy. More precisely (as John Gray suggests) it is a trade mission in which these two great economic powers make agreements which are to their mutual benefit. The narrative is a rather gloating summary of the wealth and prestige of the Israelite monarchy. The report of the trade mission was likely different for the public of Sheba.

(ii) The narrative is formed around the beginnings in vv. 1–5 and the conclusion of vv. 10–13. The beginning section (vv. 1–5) gives a reason for coming. Clearly, Solomon has succeeded beyond every expectation. The queen is impressed with his wisdom, (i.e., his managerial skills), his palace complex, his extravagant foods, his bureaucracy and its accouterments. Curiously, the description ends with a feeble affirmation of piety in v. 5. But the piety noted is conventional and belongs to the well-appointed royal household. It is only a part of the necessary royal program.

The conclusion is telling. RSV has "there was no spirit in her." It would catch the dramatic closure of the statement by reading, "it took her breath away." Solomon is not only "like the nations." He surpasses them at their own game (1 Kgs 3:13). That much is surely good royal propaganda but also a statement of Yahweh's enormous blessing.

(iii) The conclusion of vv. 10–13 reads like the joint statement issued on the last day of a summit meeting. Or perhaps it is the dramatic announcement of a new trade agreement, with benefits for both parties. We are here exposed to "reasons of state." The narrative is governed by "she gave" (v. 10) and "Solomon gave" (v. 13), the two being symmetrical. Both rulers made a gift to the other, to consolidate the agreement. The substance of the exchange is exotic, both to indicate their extraordinary affluence and to impress the citizenry. It is like the gifts given the queen of England on her tour of the Persian Gulf states, exotic beyond every practicality, but terribly important for enhancement of both regimes.

(c) But the center of preaching material is not to be found in these opening and concluding narratives which are rather mundane and conventional. Interest falls on the speech of vv. 6–9, which surprises us. There the queen responds to her surprise. And her response is a telling one.

The speech of the queen is sandwiched between the opening and concluding narrative sections. The speech is a carefully constructed one with an intentional and distinctive juxtaposition of motifs. Preaching might best focus on that juxtaposition.

(i) Vv. 6–8 are likely conventional celebration of affluence. Solomon is commended for his wisdom and his "prosperity." (The term "prosperity" translates the Hebrew word *tov*, which is often rendered "good." Here it refers to his achievements and his standard of living.) It seems likely that the queen is more overwhelmed by his *wealth* than his *wisdom*. Thus there is something of a changed agenda.

The parallel speech of v. 8 is so overdrawn as to be ironic. The double "happy" recalls the joy of 4:20. But the irony is that first the "wives" are happy. This is the Greek reading; Hebrew has "men," which would refer to his court circles of powerful officials. Reading "wives," the text refers to his harem (see 11:3). The readings are easily confused in Hebrew ("wives" = *naseka*, "men" = *anaseka*). The second parallel speaks of "servants" (slaves). The irony is that it is unlikely that either a harem of competing women or a cadre of servants (even if they are high officials) would be happy unless by "happy" is meant only physical satiation. But surely the system works. Perhaps there is enough of satisfaction to quiet every dream of freedom. In any case, vv. 6–8 are what might be expected when one monarch wants to gain the favor of any other ruler by extravagant rhetoric.

(ii) But the response of the queen continues in v. 9, which is unexpected. I take this to be a statement inappropriate to a visiting dignitary, but a quite predictable statement from one of Israel's theologians who shaped the text. Here at last is a theologically intentional affirmation. But its power is the odd way in which it relates to the rest of the unit.

Two comments are important. First, the mention of Yahweh in this intentional way is surprising. (The references to Yahweh in vv. 1, 5 are conventional and lacking the same force.) By contrast, this powerful doxological statement in the mouth of a foreigner is noteworthy. Moreover, the word "blessed" (after the double use of "happy" in v. 8) sharply shifts the topic in a theological direction. From v. 8 to v.9 is a

move from practical eudemonism to covenanted faith. Vv.
6–8 leave Israel autonomous, as though this is all *achieved.*
Now clearly the well-being of Solomon is known to be a *gift.*
This statement sets the would-be autonomous achievement
of Solomon in a context of faith (see 1 Cor 4:7). Everything is
redefined and the royal ideology of the self-made king is
sharply criticized. It is all gift!

Second, the last part of the verse introduces the double
phrase, "justice and righteousness." This is a set phrase of
covenantal theology, available for radical prophetic teaching
(see Gen 18:19; Isa 5:7; Amos 5:7, 24, 6:12, Jer 22:13, 15). It
refers to intervention by the king on behalf of the powerless,
a general alertness to social well-being for all persons in the
midst of deep social inequities.

The foundations of Israel's understanding of kingship
(which here the visiting queen understands better than the
resident king; see 1 Kgs 21:7) legitimated the institution on
the basis of justice and righteousness. This is the test of legitimate rule (see Ps 72:1, 4, Prov 8:20). This is a distinctive notion of kingship in Israel. It subordinates royal power (and
prosperity) to social awareness and responsibility. Thus v. 9
makes monarchy clearly theonomous and ethically concerned. Now the contemporary preacher will not often address kings. But the claim may be extended to every kind of
power and every form of knowledge and well-being.

V. 9, it appears to me, is a correction of a royal understanding in Jerusalem that increasingly ignored the claims of
Israel's tradition. In its present form in the mouth of the foreign queen, this text juxtaposes *the most extravagant claim of
kingship* (wisdom and prosperity) and *the most disciplined
hopes of covenanted Israel* (justice and righteousness).

And that juxtaposition is the preachable point. Then or
now, how are wisdom and prosperity related to justice and
righteousness? Or how does v. 9 relate to vv. 6–8? Is it a
faithful corrective? Is it a natural unfolding? Is it a quarrel-
some contradiction? This is the issue everyone with power
has to face. We could have expected the speech of the queen
to stop at v. 8. And we would prefer to stop there in an assessment of our own lives. But the text does not stop there. The
voice of prophetic faith is sounded here, albeit by a foreign
queen. It is made clear that the purpose of royal power is not

wisdom and prosperity, much as we prefer it. Rather, the point of all that goes before is *justice and righteousness.* And any other purpose is bound to bring failure and destruction.

Attention might be given to Jer 22:13–17, another proposal about kingship. It is worth noting that the same words occur. In Jer 22:13 there are negatives: *un*righteousness and *in*justice. In v. 15, they are positve. And in vv. 15, 16 the word "well" is used, the same word *tov* which is "prosperity" in 2 Kgs 10:7. Thus in that text as well, the question is posed about the relation of *good* ("prosperity") and *justice, righteousness.* And where there is no justice and righteousness, there will not be "prosperity."

(d) The ground for the entire narrative is Solomon's *wisdom.* As we have seen, royal wisdom is not disinterested. And so the narrative extrapolates from wisdom to success. The wisdom theme is worth pondering. It is a current question. What constitutes genuine wisdom? Is it the shrewdness to work one's way? Is it the capacity to mobilize people for corporate ends? Is it the skill to bracket out value questions and live in a way so that no serious, critical or transcendent questions can surface? Solomon came close to that. He ignored the justice and righteousness of v. 9 for the sake of the prosperity of v. 7.

So what does it mean to be wise? Two answers might be given which tell against Solomon. Nevertheless, they have urgent contemporaneity. On the one hand, the OT is unambiguous. "The fear of the Lord is the beginning of wisdom" (Prov 1:7). Real wisdom consists in attentiveness to Yahweh's purposes. Solomon's royal pretensions blinded him to this consideration. On the other hand, and more radically, the cross which the world regards as foolish is indeed the "wisdom of God" (1 Cor 1:22–25). Of course I do not suggest reading the text of 1 Kg 10:1–13 in terms of Jesus. But the issues are the same. It is *brokenness* which brings *healing.* It is *caring* for justice and righteousness which causes "good." And in the long run, any other good will come to nought (see 1 Cor 1:28). While the text may not be drawn directly to Jesus, it surely is illuminated by the claims of the gospel which are evident in both Old and New Testaments.

By considering the juxtaposition of our text in relation to 1 Cor 1:28–31, we can hear in the words of Sheba in v. 9 *a radical critique* of the royal program of vv. 6–8. It should be clear that we deal not with sharp questions raised only by preachers. Rather, we deal with the deepest questions of our faith and of life. Could it be that all the "good" in the world does not free us from anxiety? Indeed, "even Solomon in all his glory is not arrayed like one of these. . . ." "But seek first his kingdom and his righteousness, and all these things shall be yours as well" (Matt 6:29, 33). But "all these things" cannot be *grasped* first. They can only be *given* last. Solomon gives little evidence of reliance on the Father who "knows you need them all."

(5) "King Solomon excelled. . . .in riches and in wisdom" (10:11–29). And we may believe he did even better at riches than at wisdom. Israel, only a few generations from the poverty and precariousness of the hill country, could not cease to marvel at this incredible movement from "rags to riches." And Israel could not help but see it as a gift from God. The consciousness of Israel (or at least of Solomon and the people around him) may have been like that of Middle America, fresh from depression, or memories of immigration, people who now have made it, but who can hardly believe it. And as a result, they do not know when to stop. In recent American history, it is such a skewed conscience, embodied, for example, in Lyndon Johnson and Richard Nixon, which powered the savage Viet Nam effort. There was no one who knew when enough of exploitation was enough. And there must always be more. So Solomon excelled. He had more—and more—and more!

(a) His trade agreement with Hiram (see 5:12) brought endless goods (10:11–12). And Solomon is like shopping for someone who has everything. There was nothing left for him to purchase or confiscate.

(b) Solomon dazzled the queen of Sheba (10:13, see vv. 1–10). Perhaps she was his only counterpart and social peer. He is indeed number 1, just as the narrative presents him.

(c) Gold, gold, gold, gold, gold—with a little ivory, and some exotic apes and peacocks (vv. 14–22)! One cannot tell if this is a bored man who has it continually come in long after he has lost interest. Or is he is still a passionate entrepreneur for whom *getting* is more satisfying than *having*. Obviously he had to keep escalating the art forms of his city. They became extravagant, bizarre and eventually utterly gauche. Perhaps by that time no one was any longer impressed, except the others who played the same game. Israel's kings were warned about silver, gold, chariots, horses and wives (Deut 17:14–17). All of that is a dead end. But Solomon scarcely studied the torah enough to know about the warning (see Deut 17:18–20). There was no time for study, and surely no inclination.

(d) It is all a story of unmitigated success (10:23–29). People made pilgrimages of disbelief. They discovered that the real thing outstripped their rumors and their imagination. This is the quintessence of technical and managerial efficiency in which the rich get richer and richer, even to utter alienation.

Perhaps it is important that the narrator reports all this dispassionately, even objectively. There is no excitement about it, also no criticism. Solomon is scarcely a cause for celebration here. It may be that the narrator believes that such conspicuous consumption carries its own commentary, that the absurdity of it all is evident in the telling of it.

Or perhaps the placement of this account between 9:1–9 and 11:1–13 makes the point. The "if . . . then" of 9:1–9 concerns torah obedience. 11:1–13 exposes the deathliness of the system of aggrandizement. All of it together is a muted but decisive commentary that Solomon is pursuing a course to death. The destructiveness is not found in personal lust and covetousness. We have no hint of Solomon's personal passions, for that is not the problem. No. The matter is more systemic. It is the forming of a system of lust larger than any person. One has the impression that Solomon is only a figure head. Without him the system could perhaps go on amassing more wealth at the expense of "the others." If one can be freed of a personalistic reading of Solomon, one might use this report as a mirror for our own economic tyranny. Our society is increasingly better off. That is unarguable. But none of us knows it or limits it. None of us sees the poor who finance all this wealth with their bodies. It may give pause that this congratulatory report is only two chapters removed from the resistance movement of chapter 12.

A variety of New Testament linkages come to mind. Three may be noted:

(1) Solomon may be the embodiment of the man in Luke 12:13–21 who tears down his barn to build bigger barns. He had been deceived into thinking that abundance of possessions is the substance of a man's life. And Solomon is indeed a "man of substance" if anything. The inescapable voice in the night says "fool." And then the voice makes an ultimate requirement (Luke 12:20).

(2) Paul to Corinth puts the key question to Solomonic folks: "What do you have that you did not receive?" (1 Cor 4:7–8). What of all of this is an achievement and not a gift? And Paul's implied answer does not surprise us: NOTHING. But that is always a surprise in our Solomonic self-assuredness.

(3) Perhaps most decisively, Jesus' teaching to his disciples in the Sermon on the Mount is a terse statement about God and *"capital"* (Matt 6:24). And then there follows a statement about *anxiety*. I submit that Solomon was the utterly anxious man. And his anxiety is what drove the economic machine. In the center of that teaching (Matt 6:25–33), Jesus delivers a striking comment on our text:

> "Even Solomon in all his glory, is not arrayed like one of these."

Even Solomon! Especially Solomon! And then this: "Your heavenly father knows."

The preacher may seek to penetrate behind the economic drives for success and security. As Hannah Arendt can speak of the "banality of evil," so we can speak of the banality of such consumptive greed. It does not hold our interest very long. At the root of it is our fear of death, our need for self-security, our penchant for being noticed and taken seriously. Could a "gospel of graciousness" disengage us from the hopeless enterprise of self-security? It's an interesting question, both for the preacher and for the congregation.

On Loving More Than One Thing (11:1–13)

Solomon is a mirror for us in our life of faith. What we are able to discern in Solomon we know so well about ourselves. And that is how the text was originally intended. It was not shaped as it is, simply to give an historical report about a tenth-century king. Rather, it is offered so that Israel could see more perceptively what is happening in its midst—in every generation.

The narrative about Solomon (1 Kgs 3–11) contains sound historical materials about the king's rule and his administration. But our text (together with 3:3) stands as an envelope at the beginning and end of the report. They serve to frame the narrative and to suggest a certain perspective on the Solomonic material. It is possible to take these two notices chronologically. In that way, 3:3 tells about his good faith at the beginning. And 11:1–3 tells of his bad faith at the end. Read in that way, Solomon's life is the story of erosion and deterioration, so that we see a powerful man going "to the dogs."

But these verses need not be understood chronologically. It could be that the two options of 3:3 and 11:1–13 are the context and extremities of the life and faith. And we are always moving between them, i.e., between love of the Lord and love of other loyalties. Thus each day, soon and late, young and old, in season and out of season, we are always choosing between these two loves. Or conversely, we are always trying to escape the choice, so that we can have it both ways. The terse statement of Jesus in Matt 6:24 summarizes the extended presentation of Solomon. And the pastoral task is to help people understand the tricky place where we live, between these alternatives and the dangerous choices that must be made daily.

(1) We first meet Solomon (3:3) in a posture of serious faith: he loved the Lord. It is a simple, unqualified statement, showing an unambiguous intent. Such an absence of ambiguity surely is a source of energy and authority. In that moment, Solomon is a man of pure heart, for he does will only one thing. Now such a notion may strike us as simplistic or irrelevant in our complicated situation. But a sermon might help people focus on the simple claims of faith which need not be made inordinately complex. People in our society need help in thinking about love of the Lord which is to be more than a religious cliché. I have recently been reading *Lest Innocent Blood Be Shed*, an account of Le Chambeau, a French village which acted in bold ways under its pastor, Andre Trocme in the Second World War. In quiet and determined ways, they provided protection for Jews at great risk.

But it is neither spectacular or complicated. It was a simple love of the gospel which permitted bold, uncomplicated acts of faithfulness. But such simple boldness requires a decision about priorities and first loves. The people of Le Chambeau resolved simply to do what the gospel required.

(a) It has been shown that the word love *(ahab)* in some contexts, perhaps here, means "to honor covenant commitments." That is, love is not an emotional matter, but it is the acknowledgment of a formal relationship in which both parties have obligations to each other. For Solomon, to love Yahweh means to be clear about God's expectations and to order life to meet those expectations. This provides an opportunity to reflect on God's expectations for those with whom He has covenant. See John 14:21, where love of God is also equated with obedience to commandments.

(b) The term "love" here reflects the injunction of Deut 6:5 to love Yahweh with all the heart, all the person and all the power at our disposal. That is, the teaching calls for a massive self-surrender to the subject of one's love. But it is important that in Deuteronomy, the word "love" belongs in a cluster of other words which have a different nuance about them: fear, walk in his ways, serve, obey, cleave (see 10:12, 13:4). That is, this love is not simply a religious element in life, but it is a drastic reorientation of all of life.

(c) But the text further presses the covenant one to a surrender that is both massive and concrete. In our text as well as in Deuteronomy (see 6:6, 10:13, 13:4), it is clear that *love means obedience*. The intention of a right heart must be given concrete expression. A sermon might address the temptation we currently have to separate love and obedience in our culture, or even to make them antithetical. Biblical faith is not a collection of good intentions or right attitudes. It deals with concrete acts.

Of course, it will be asked if love can be commanded. And the answer is, "no," if love is understood as emotion and command as coercion, for emotion cannot be coerced. But love is not emotion, but loyalty. And command is not coercion, but the hopes of a respected and trusted partner. And so the love God wills can be commanded in the liberating way that God commands.

The "love-command" on which our text is premised is

carried into the NT. It is evident in Jesus' summary of the torah concerning love of God and of neighbor (Mark 12:28–31). And it is clear in the meditation of John 15:12–17. Love of God means to honor the *holiness of God* and to respect the *justice of the neighbor.* Our text asserts that Solomon is a model for such fidelity. And our text affirms that even in our kind of world, such a simple and overriding loyalty is possible.

(2) But 3:3 is not naive. Already here in this initial, celebrative verse, there is a qualifying footnote: Only he still practiced an alternative religion; he sacrificed at the high places. If only v. 3a could be the whole statement. But it is not, for Solomon or for us. There is here a "reserve clause" that must be presented even in this commendation of Solomon.

His utter loyalty to Yahweh already here includes a mitigating factor. The king could not bring himself to yield on this point. The sermon can move into the dark reality of our love for God, but observing as the Bible knows so well, we will qualify that love just a bit whenever we can.

The "high places" refer to an alternative religious practice. The theory behind this narrative is that true worship, orthodox and faithful, is only done in Jerusalem. And that required the closing of all other sanctuaries where doubtful, undisciplined religion is practiced. But even the king, that great model of fidelity, has not gotten his loyalties unified. The "high places" are an attempt to keep an option open, not quite to bring it all under the single rubric of covenant. So the sermon might reflect on the "reserve clauses" we all prefer, in religion and economics, in psychology and politics, to withhold just a little from the sovereign rule of God.

This part of the verse is only an afterthought in the narrative. Nothing is made of it. In 3:4–14, the story ignores the qualification and goes on to celebrate the loyalty. But the clue is dropped. And the knowing observer will watch for it to reappear. The narrator is realistic. If such a qualifier is evident so early in the plot, it holds the possibility of an utterly compromised faith. And that, of course, is offered in chapter 11.

(3) We can move readily from the beginning (3:3a) to the reserve clause (3:3b) to the end (11:1–13). That reserve clause

of withheld loyalty now comes to fruition. There is irony
here. The same word, "love," is used in 11:1, repeated in v. 3.
Perhaps this formula suggests a sad end to an otherwise glo-
rious life. I prefer to think the narrator knows that 11:1–13 is
always a present temptation, always an alternative to 3:3, always an inclination to reduce our life and divide our
loyalties.

(a) It is the same word, "love," which we saw in 3:3. Love
is not a spiritual or emotional word here, either. Again, it refers to covenanting loyalty. It is definitional that covenant
loyalty must be undivided. And here it is divided, many
times over. And that means that covenantal love is hopeless-
ly betrayed and perverted.

(b) The new religious alternative is "many foreign wom-
en." Undoubtedly, there is a sexual dimension to his perver-
sity—such a dimension, 300 wives and 700 concubines! But
we should not be misled. The point is not sexual, but political. The many marriages and the harem are a way to imple-
ment international alliances. And all of these efforts in the
sexuality of politics and the politicization of sexuality are
ways to secure one's own existence, to retain initiative for
one's life. And the upshot is to eliminate the transcendent
Lord and any principle of criticism. Solomon's new, alternative loves have reduced life to something manageable, predictable and administrable. To love God means to yield
before One who is an overwhelming holy mystery. It is to
trust but not be in control. Conversely, to have these modest,
divided loves is to love only as much as we can manage and
so to be in control. That is the temptation which the lovers of
this God have always faced.

(c) It is clear that the narrator has no interest in the
many women as such. By v. 2, the love is not of the women,
but of the "other gods." Thus the mention of wives and concubines is quickly shown for what it is, a religious alternative
which means the betrayal of the primal commitments of
3:3a. Thus the reserve claim of 3:3b has become decisive.

Solomon ends up with the worst kind of heart trouble
(cf. vv. 4, 9). His heart can no longer believe the promises and
so cannot run the necessary risks. The new condition of his
heart is not pure, and he will not draw near to God as he did
in Gibeon (see 1 Kgs 3:4–13, Matt 5:8). Solomon's heart fol-

lowed his treasure (Matt 6:21) which is a treasure soon to be lost (1 Kgs 11:11).

(d) Finally, it should be noted that the divided loyalty of Solomon and the settlement of the two conflicting loves is not only a religious matter. This text knows that social behavior follows our religion. How we treat the neighbor is closely linked to the God we love. The one who *turned from Yahweh* became a *social oppressor*. The demise of his kingdom happened not by direct intervention of God, but by social unrest among those who would not abandon their freedom (1 Kgs 11:28, 12:40). Finally, the two commandments will not be separated. Who does not love God surely cannot love neighbor (1 John 4:2). And when we cannot love neighbor, we lose all we have been given.

These texts are a way to identify and reassess the practice of faith in a context of unresolved ambiguity. That is where loyalty is always at issue.

The Irresistible Word in the Face of Royal Guarantees (11:14–43)

Solomon may indeed have been a great and effective king, as presented in 9:10—10:29. But this narrator knows something else about Solomon, something more important. He knows Solomon is sitting on a time-bomb of disobedience. The narrator is not seduced by the criteria of the world. The king who appears to be prospering in every way is in fact in deep danger. Human power is to be assessed differently because of God's sovereign will. No king or any power agent is ever so blessed as to be immune from the expectations of the torah. The narrator thus submits this entire regime, powerful and impressive as it is, to the simple, unambiguous norm of the Torah.

(1) Vv. 1–8 appear to be narrative. But in fact these verses are a standard prophetic indictment. They specify the ways in which this king has violated torah, precisely because the king imagined himself immune from these old and seemingly irrelevant standards and expectations.

(a) The key indictment (v. 1) is, as we have seen, structurally parallel to 3:3. These are the options before the king: love of the Lord/love of foreign women. These loves are mutually exclusive. One cannot have it both ways (see Matt

6:24). Eventually one must choose, or unwittingly one will find one has already chosen. Solomon did choose. And his choice turned out to be deathly (see Deut 30:15–20).

(b) The love of foreign women is not primarily a sexual affront. Rather these marriage arrangements are political settlements. They are expressions of a network of alliances designed to give national security. Solomon is here under indictment not for personal lust, but because of his hopeless efforts at self-security. He imitates "the ways of the nations." And whenever the nations are imitated, other loyalties displace a singular loyalty to Yahweh. So the real issue is that Solomon's heart is turned from the Lord (vv. 2, 4). Solomon had grasped after the treasures of the nations. And his heart followed his treasure (Matt 5:21). The norm for Israel is an undivided heart given to Yahweh (Deut 6:5). And now Solomon's heart is divided, toward Yahweh but also toward efforts at self-security which do not believe Yahweh is enough.

(c) The result is of course religious syncretism (vv. 5–8). And with such distorted religion, everything else becomes distorted as well. Solomon exchanged the truth about God for a lie (Rom 1:25). Solomon's regime increasingly came to reflect and embody these new, illicit loyalties (Hos 9:10). The pursuit of worthlessness leads here to worthlessness (Jer 2:5). Solomon succeeded in shifting the foundations of society. One cannot choose between social policy and personal religion of the heart. One cannot bracket out the one from the other. They belong together and will inevitably influence each other. Solomon's personal life is simply one facet of his larger public, ambiguous commitments. And in the process he had forfeited his trust from God. He had begun as a young king to whom God has entrusted everything. But now the trust is in jeopardy, and is recalled by God from the king.

(2) Solomon was not without warning. There had been two dreams (vv. 9–10; cf. 3:5–14, 9:1–9). One should be on notice if a dream has a threatening sequel. The second dream concerns us here. It is a harsh truth-telling dream. It announces that power and privilege are conditional. The second dream had best not be ignored.

(3) So the narrative moves in predictable fashion from the *indictment* of vv. 1–8 to the *sentence* of vv. 11–13. This is

not easy material to proclaim in the American church. But
that makes it no less pertinent. It was not easy in ancient
Israel either. But it is not a statement of blustering hostility
from God. Rather it is a cold, sober recognition of how life
works. Violation of torah leads to trouble, soon or late. This
narrative has unflinching confidence in the rule of God
which will not be mocked. Not even the powerful can circumvent the torah of Yahweh. Finally there will be a reckon-
ing, even among the great ones (see Isa 10:13–14). Thus
history moves to a "therefore." Just now Americans are left
to wonder about the "therefore" which follows self-indulgent
prosperity, for the "therefore" now is loose in the world in
various, irresistible and frightening ways.

(a) The sentence of v. 11 is simple, clear and directive.
Violation of torah leads to loss of power. This was clear already in 3:14. And that may be the real energy crisis.

(b) But vv. 12–13 is candid on a troublesome point. Solomon should have been denied power. But he was not denied.
He died a safe and respectable death, full of years. And the
reason? Why was certain judgment stayed? In the inscrutable ways of God, we do not know. But our theologian juxtaposes the *guilt of Solomon* and the *merit of David*. In the short
run, for just now, "David's sake" prevails. It is a temporary
stay, but nonetheless gratefully received. Historically this is
simply a recognition of political fact. Theologically the mercy of God struggles with the exhausted patience of God.

But even with such qualifications of delay and limit, this
is a striking statement of judgment in royal history. We
should not expect such a hostile, negative judgment to occur
in a royal account. But this is not simply royal narrative. It is
rather a report on the way of the torah. Devastatingly and
without apology, this historian understands torah to be the
ultimate, unavoidable power of the historical process. And
no royal cleverness or calculation can work around it.

(4) The remainder of the chapter is an implementation of
this heavy, unexpected judgment (vv. 14–43).

(a) Solomon is surrounded by suppressed people waiting
to have their vengeance at the first sign of weakness. The first
move is made by the kingdom of Edom (vv. 14–23). The treatment of Edom by David and Joab (vv. 15–16) sounds like an
anticipation of the "Slaughter of the Innocents" (Matt 2:16).

And of course that abuse evoked enduring resentment, a long, determined memory.

Egypt (the same government which harbored the Shah of Iran more recently) is the refuge for the government of Edom in exile. Solomon sits on a powder keg. Solomon is presented here as a ruthless exploiter. Nothing comes of this narrative. But it makes clear that David had bequeathed to his heir and dynasty a back log of hatred, crying for retaliation.

(b) Of the second opponent (Rezon, vv. 23–25), we are not told much. Again it is David whose ruthless ways evoke the hostility.

(5) But the narrative is primarily interested in the internal threat of Jeroboam (vv. 26–40). This is the serious danger which finally makes the difference. The preacher might pause with the hint here that *internal* threats have a way of danger not shared on the outside.

(a) Jeroboam is a member of Solomon's bureaucracy, in charge of state labor policy (vv. 26–28). We are not told more than that. Did he flinch from the oppression? Was he a popular government figure around which opposition to the king could rally?

(b) We do not know. But Jeroboam draws the attention of the prophet (vv. 29–31). So we do not know about *political* factors. The narrator has it that the *prophetic* impetus is the decisive factor. Jeroboam may be other things, but here he is simply a tool of God's judgment of David's house. The *dynasty* cannot resist the *word*. No earthly arrangement of power is ultimate, innocent or safe. This royal history is in fact a child of the disruptive word of God. And that word is unimpressed and undeterred by the ways of royal claim and royal pretense.

(c) As in vv. 12–13, the narrative (here as prophetic speech) speaks the truth, showing that the judgment now given is neither immediate nor total. On the one hand, the judgment is qualified by leaving Judah (vv. 32, 36). On the other hand, the judgment is delayed a generation, permitting Solomon to die a safe death (v. 34). But that changes things only slightly and not essentially.

(d) Kings come and go. But the Word watches over its people (see Jer 1:11–12). So the threat against Solomon con-

stitutes the authorization of Jeroboam (vv. 37–40). And this
is a surprising thing to find in the books of Kings. We expect
that any northern king should be a usurper, denounced in
principle. And in every other case that is the situation. But
not here. Here the would-be usurper is legitimate. The promise made to the rebel is as full as that made to Solomon. On
the one hand, the same condition of torah is given, but it is
not more than required of Solomon (see 3:14). And in any
case, it is assumed that this northern king can and will keep
the torah. There is here no prejudgment that the torah cannot or will not be kept by this king. Not much is made of it,
but the possibility is as radical as the later "good Samari-
tan," also a northerner regarded as an outsider. This renegade from the north will do more faithfully than this special
family of the Jerusalem crown.

And on the other hand, the promise is fully dynastic. It is
to be a "sure house," as sure as that promised to David (see 2
Sam 7:16). The possibility of a legitimated northern dynasty
is entertained. And briefly it comes to fruition (12:15). The
word has its way midst the treacheries of royal intrigue. Sad-
ly, the narrator does not return to this high hope for the
north. And by 12:25–33, the northern dynasty is roundly and
unequivocally condemned. Rather strangely, Solomon under
such sentence is permitted a good death (vv. 41–43).

Preaching in this text can be done at the point of deep
incongruity: the great king—the shattering word; high powered government—helpless against the resilient torah. Kings
may devise and scheme and secure themselves. But soon or
late they must answer and give account of themselves (see
Prov 16:9, 21). Against the greatness of Solomon, there is
only the word of this Ahijah without credentials. But the
wind of God blows where it will. And no king can stop its
blowing.

An Interlude
(1 Kings 12:1—16:34)

This portion of the text may be regarded as an interlude in the literature. It stands between 1 Kings 3–11 (on Solomon) and 1 Kings 17–2 Kings 10:36 (on the revolution of the northern prophets). As the text is now arranged, this position is primarily *transitional*.

But of course that is a literary shaping. When one considers the upheaval of this period in Israel's history from 922 B.C. (the death of Solomon) to 869 (the beginning of Ahab's reign), it is clearly a time of disorder, war and the emergence of new configurations of power. Thus the *literary shaping* suggests a quite distinct perspective on historical events. As elsewhere, we do not have here simply an historical presentation, but a *theological judgment* about the meaning of events, according to the overriding purposes of God.

This odd grouping of texts includes:
   (a) a report of political schism (12:1–16),
   (b) the founding of an alternative shrine (12:25–33),
   (c) a tale of conflicting prophets (13:1–32),
   (d) a narrative on the sickness of a king (14:1–16) and,
   (e) a royal reform (15:9–15).
In addition the text is built around stylized and repetitious judgments about various kings.

A Hope Allied with the Hopeless Ones (12:1–24)

The death of Solomon in 922 B.C. made a new beginning possible. At the end of his reign, Solomon had become oppressive (11:26–28). But the son need not continue in the oppression of the father. (See Ezek 18 on the possibility that the new generation need not be locked into the parental modes.) The son had a chance to take new initiatives in the direction of humanness which the father had long neglected. Thus a great deal is at stake in this constitutional convention at Shechem. Shechem was a traditional meeting place for the old confederation (Josh 24:1). It was a place where Israel assembled when something crucial was to be decided. Rehoboam, son of Solomon, will be king. But the order and shape and character of his monarchy is still to be determined. It is not automatic. He can, unlike his father, choose life (see Deut 30:15–20). But he must bargain and negotiate and take account of agendas other than his own (vv. 1–5).

(1) Discussion among his royal advisors produced two conflicting pieces of advice. His old advisors, the ones who had lived longer, seen more and remembered most, counseled conciliation (vv. 6–7). Perhaps they understood how precarious is the throne. The young upstarts, new to government and flushed with power which seemed to have no limit, advised new, harsher measures (vv. 8–11). They understood little about the nature of power and authority and the peculiar impact of consent witheld or given.

The issue facing Rehoboam, and everyone with power over others, concerns the shape of power and the nature of authority. There is something inscrutable about effective power and authority which is never to be reduced to brute force. The Christian Gospel is about another kind of power which works in irresistible ways but never by brute force or by compulsion. This narrative poses for us questions about power, authority and force, power aimed at humanness which need not appeal to force and power flatly equated with force. Note well, the cycle of force is not begun by the subjects but by the king.

(2) Rehoboam chose wrongly (vv. 12–20). The narrative is unambiguous about it. The young king listened to those who thought royal power was unlimited and answerable to none (shades of "Watergate"; vv. 12–14). And in making that choice, the future of Israel was dangerously shaped. "Once to every man and nation comes the moment to decide". . . and he blew it!

(a) The offer of oppressive kingship is rejected. Israel remembered too much and wanted no more of it. But as our narrator sees it, this was clearly in the cards (v. 15). The prophet to Solomon (Ahijah) had already anticipated the alienation of the north (11:29–35). The oppression of the son brought it to reality.

(b) Israel was able to remember an alternative form of public power. So the defiant cry of v. 16 recalls the old

premonarchial order of things (see 2 Sam 20:24). The king
might not know it. But kingship in Israel is a luxury, not a
necessity: "Got along without it before I met you, gonna' get
along without it now." Kingship is not definitional for Israel.
As Israel got along without monarchy in the beginning, so it
will now. Every public arrangement of power is tentative
and therefore the seeds of deep change in Israel are always
present. No present ordering of church or the civil community, or even of a person's self-characterization, is essential.

(c) Rehoboam learned only a little. And he learned that
very late. He proceeded with oppressive labor policy, repli-
cating his father's odious and self-destructive practice (vv.
17–20). And in the end, he got only more rebellion. There is
not enough force to down the yearning for freedom. The upshot was an alternative form of power in the north, set up
around the popular Jeroboam who had been exiled by Solomon to Egypt (v. 2). As the price of his grandiose schemes
and foolish counsel toward imperial oppression, Rehoboam
lost most of his patrimony. And the conflict between the lost
part and the retained part was to continue until there was
nothing more about which to fight.

(3) The anticipation of Ahijah in 11:29–35 came to fruition. So our narrative traces the strange alliance between the
word of God (which foretold the collapse) and the *cause of
justice* among the oppressed. This theologian believes the
Word is allied with the *powerless*, against the regime. Indeed
it is only the word which acts for the powerless and which
keeps check on the unbridled power of an irresponsible, unre-
sponsive king. It is this alliance which is fundamental to this
presentation of history. And to be faithful we are not permitted to separate them, word and justice, to have the word
without attention to the powerless, nor to care for the powerless without the overriding bouyancy of the word. Thus we
can think of this fundamental linkage in various places in the
tradition:

(a) Isa 57:15—The high and lofty one in eternity dwells
with the humble and contrite of heart.
(b) Prov 17:5—Who mocks the poor insults the creator.
(c) Luke 7:20–23—The test of Jesus' messianic claim is
his effective solidarity with the needful.

Rehoboam's utter miscalculation, premised on a mis-
reading of Israel's faith and a misconception of power, was

that he could be a king "like the nations" (1 Sam 8:5, 20). He was not aware that power in Israel is of another kind.

(4) The narrator adds a curious note in vv. 21–24. Rehoboam was ready to respond to the secession in the only way he knew—by armed power. With enough arms, a king ought to be able to do what he wills. And yet, says the narrator, even Rehoboam is subject to the prophetic word. Even this cynical agent of power politics cannot finally circumvent this other inscrutable Power who makes history. Even this insensitive military machine is penetrated. Even in the dynastic south with its crass self-serving, God's word will have its say. Presumably Rehoboam with his dynastic, bureaucratic strength, could have crushed the popular movement of the north. But God's word would not have it so. The hidden move for justice in the world is an oddity. It is hard to know how or why the "refugee movements" in our world are not finally crushed. Why is it the Palestinians still hope toward justice, or that Blacks in South Africa have not quit? Undoubtedly more than one reading is possible. But in this text the pseudo-legitimacy of dynastic power is checked by nothing less (and nothing more) than God's word. And that word is from time to time enfleshed against the powers that be. For just now, it is God's purpose that the breakaway movement should have its time for a new beginning. For just now, it is seen to be a "sanctioned" rebellion.

A most obvious preaching point in this text is that the "American way" in the world does not have full sway. There are counter movements in the world which threaten and frighten. We must take care that in such movements, God's relentless commitment to justice may work against us as it did against the regime in Jerusalem. Less directly, this same text may give access to power questions closer home, to ask about power arrangements in domestic situations and the ways in which the voice of freedom and justice will not be silenced. Each of us experiences rebellions against our fragile orderliness. This text invites a pause, that the sway of God may be on the other side of the issue.

Home-made Religion (12:25–33)

Our narrator does not miss the strange contradiction and irony in the history of Israel. In 12:1–24, he has appreciated Jeroboam as the rallying point against dynastic oppression. In that episode Jeroboam is ordained of God and is the key figure in a liberation movement. But the narrator has no wish to celebrate Jeroboam as a hero of faith. Thus what he commends in vv. 1–24, in vv. 25–33 he condemns out of hand.

(1) Jeroboam, claimant of a rival regime, is in a tight place. He has a popular political following. But he cannot sustain this loyalty unless he has a visible form of religious legitimacy. And that legitimacy cannot come from Jerusalem, the most legitimate of all places, for the Jerusalem establishment is owned and operated by his southern enemy. So this chapter is about the need and problem of *religious legitimacy* for a would-be liberation movement. A sermon might reflect on the matter of religious legitimacy. What needs to happen for a movement to claim religious legitimacy? How does it happen? Who grants it? How may it be lost or at least placed in jeopardy? One might reflect on civil religion in America, on the "usefulness" of the church to the corporate economy and its quest for religious legitimacy. Alternatively, one may ask about the movements for justice and freedom which tend to be or claim to be religious movements. And what separates authentic and fake legitimacy?

(2) It is the argument of this narrative that the entire claim for legitimacy in the north by Jeroboam is false and without authority or power. Indeed, the "sin of Jeroboam" is seen as decisive for the entire history of the north that follows (see 2 Kings 17:22–23). Jeroboam is at the same time *the voice of critical liberation* against the regime (positively handled) and the *initiator of fraudulent religious legitimacy* (condemned by the narrator). In the end, his movement must fail and can only bring trouble. The negative judgment of vv. 25–33 overrides the positive anticipation of vv. 1–24.

(3) The narrative focuses unrelievedly on the nature of the legitimacy which is sure to fail:

(a) The rival objects (note: not subjects) of loyalty are *gold* (v. 28). That is, they are artifacts of royal pretense. (See Deut 17:17, which warns against the royal temptation to gold.) They are an embodiment of the royal concern to impress and to practice conspicuous consumption. Moreover they are *calves*, i.e., they are embodiments of fertility religion, the notion that the gift of life is within our power and we can secure ourselves by our own resources. And to these *gold calves* are wrongly assigned the proper liberating functions of Yahweh (v. 28). Yahweh, a God who is never caught in gold and never identified with fertility, is the only God with power to save. But this is an attempt to "package" the liberating God in ways that control and manipulate. Of course it will not work. This narrative in some way is linked to Exodus 32 and Aaron's golden calf. In that narrative, the God of Sinai is too radical. He is known in his holy demands and in his holy absence. But Israel yearns for a god who is nearer and not so demanding (Exod 32:1). The calf in Exod 32 and here is an attempt to reduce the danger of Yahweh. Both Aaron and Jeroboam seek to reduce Yahweh to administratable size.

(b) The priesthood formed around these new shrines is an innovation which breaks with the tradition of the Levites (v. 31). The Levites (here rejected) are the faithful champions of the faith of Moses (Exod 32:25–29). The Levites are the teachers and faithful interpreters of the torah, which focuses on Yahweh's exclusive sovereignty. But Jeroboam does not want a religion that centers in obedience. He wants to create a religion for himself (i.e., make alternative gods) which does not insist on obedience. Thus an illegitimate priesthood with no hint of Yahweh's sanction serves to compromise Yahweh's jealous claim on Israel. An alternative priesthood can tell king and people precisely what they want to learn.

(c) A regular refrain is that Jeroboam *made all this*:

"He set one. . ." (v. 29).
"He made high places. . .and appointed priests. . ."
     (v. 31).
"He appointed a feast. . ." (v. 32).
"He placed in Bethel. . ." (v. 32).
All this "he had devised in his own heart. . ." (v. 33).

It is all a religion made in his own royal image, after his own likeness, to serve his own ends. On this self-made, self-serving religion, see the caricature of Isa 44:9–20. Note also Luke 18:11, the man "prayed thus with himself." Jeroboam proposes in fact that Israel should worship "thus with himself." This is a god which is no god but it fulfills all the formal requirements without costing anything.

Jeroboam has created a religion which reflects only himself
and the needs and interests of his enterprise. In fact it is no
religion at all, but a charade of his political program. Such a
self-made religion cannot help and cannot save. For when one
cries to such a god, heaven is closed and there is only a feeble
shadow of ourselves (see Deut 32:37–38, 1 Kings 18:26–29).
Jeroboam has created a public religion without power to
save, with no transcendent principle, with no God who has
real freedom either for life or for death.

This narrative understands the awful dilemma of serious
religion. On the one hand, to really matter God must be *free*.
On the other hand, God is important only because God is *present*.
But God's freedom is too dangerous. And so we fashion
a safer religion we can administer. And we end with a hoax.
So the narrator concluded, the fate of Israel was sealed that
day, for real politics must have genuine religious legitimacy
from a real God. And no self-made substitute will do. Religion
concerning the liberating God of the Exodus (v. 28) cannot
be reduced to political ideology or psychological self-
serving. The sorry tale of the Northern Kingdom is learning
that the hard way.

Prophetic Authority and Prophetic Betrayal (13:1–32)

This is in any case a most unusual story. It is even more
so when we remember that this is the book of *Kings*. But then
it is not really a book of Kings. It purports to be about kings,
but it is in fact about *prophets*. The narrative, by the material
included, means to announce that the key factors in the history of Israel are never the rulers and governors, the people
who appear to be in charge. Rather, they are figureheads,
while the real action is with the prophets, the wild, irrevoca-
ble outsiders who always surprise and confound. This text
requires us to think quite differently about historical reality.
We are so easily seduced into thinking the "rulers of this
age" are important. Against such a domesticated view, this
narrative simply asserts (without argument) that *the word of
God has its own way*. Whatever else might be done in preaching from this text, the foundational point is that the real action is not where it seems to be.

(1) The first part of the story (vv. 1–10) firmly establishes

the authority of the prophet over against the king. It is by the command of the Lord (and no other authority) that the prophet confronts the king (v. 1). The text offers a chance for a dramatic portrayal. The prophet delivers a frontal attack on the altar just built (see 12:25–33). The altar upon which the regime is premised is declared to be scandalous and illegitimate, under judgment and sure to be destroyed (vv. 2–3).

(a) In attacking the altar, the prophet strikes at the symbolic center of the regime. It is like burning the flag, denouncing motherhood, berating the "free-market system." The text suggests how tenacious are the symbols which keep the governing regime in power. Of course it is treason. So the king tries to have the prophet arrested (v. 4). Undoubtedly the king thought he was dealing with a "communist" who would undermine all of civil order.

(b) There is a play here on the phrase "hand of the king." "Hand" here may literally refer to the physical extremity of the person of the king. But it is also a metaphor for royal power (see Jer 38:4). So to "extend the hand" means to assert the authority of the throne through proper officers. So the question is posed. What about the hand/power of the king? Is it stronger than the prophet? Can the royal authority withstand the onslaught of the prophet? Can the king silence or dispose of the prophet? So reflect on the king's hand:

> It is extended for the purpose of arrest (v. 4).
> It is dried up (v. 4).
> The prophet is asked to restore (v. 5).
> By the work of the prophet, the king's hand is made whole (v. 6).

Royal power depends on the approval and sanction of the prophet. Apart from the prophet, the king is in fact powerless, without an effective hand.

This dramatic exchange shows that things are not as they may seem. The king's power, surrounded by official palaver and all the emblems of power, is in fact nothing. And the prophetic word which seems so tenuous is in fact the real power which destroys and restores the king.

(c) The king is no dummy. He recognizes this amazing power and wants to use it. He seeks to befriend and co-opt the prophet (v. 7). But the prophet is the model of faithful obedience to his mandate. He remembers what God has commanded (vv. 8–9). He will not have his head turned by such seductions. He will do nothing to violate God's command (see Matt 4:1–11).

Thus the story is bounded by the *word/command of Yahweh* in vv. 1 and 9. Everything takes place between the two. The life of the prophet and the authority of the king are bracketed by that affirmation. And the result is that the hearers of the text are invited to reexamine the power they have taken for granted. The structure of the text suggests how fragile is the hand of the king and how God's intentions finally will not be resisted or bought off.

People in the congregation are not isolated individuals. We are all children of a system which has formed us and to which we give allegiance. This text raises questions about every system of meaning and power. Things are not settled and sure, and anyone who counts too heavily on the apparent power of the ordained order of social life will be surprised if not dismayed. Life is not settled. It is precarious and open to question. And when the system of meaning and power violates God's will, the very system itself will, soon or late, wither and fade (see Isa 40:7–8), even like the hand of the king.

> Our little systems have their day;
> They have their day and cease to be;
> They are but broken lights of thee,
> And thou, O Lord, art more than they.

So questions can be raised:

> Where do we locate legitimate authority in our world?
> How is that authority symbolized?
> What voices of dissent might be raised against a regime in revolt against God?
> What are the prophetic voices which might wither the hand of our favorite systems?

These are not irrelevant questions in our time. Many of the "king's hands" seem at the present time to be paralyzed, if not withered.

(2) Through v. 10, the prophet acquitted himself honorably and well. But the story becomes more curious in vv. 11–32. The prophet of vv. 1–10 had obeyed and was on his way home. But he is *seduced by another prophet* who now leads him into disobedience by lying to him about God's will.

And the upshot of that exchange is that the first prophet is held accountable for his disobedience, even though he was seduced and tricked by the second prophet. The result is that the prophet who first obeyed (vv. 1–10) and who now disobeyed (vv. 11–23) is destroyed (vv. 24–25). The irony is that the dead prophet is grieved by the second prophet, the very one who instigated his death (vv. 29–30).

The intent of the text is not obvious. The point of the text, if we can rightly recognize it, may be quite subtle for preaching. Things were clearer in vv. 1–10. There a prophet *vis à vis a king* is unambiguous. He is the model of obedience and will not be taken in by the advances of the king. But *vis à vis another prophet*, things get muddy. What was so clear in the first episode is now unclear. What had seemed like the full authority of the prophet is now clouded by the counter authority of another prophet who claims also to be sent by God with a contrary word (v. 18). In such a quandry, even this most faithful prophet falls into disobedience (vv. 21–22).

No motive is given for the deception of v. 18. We are not explicitly told that the second prophet is mandated by God, but that is his claim. Nor is there any hint that he was wrong or immoral. He is not at all condemned by the narrator. The narrator does not really raise such a probing question about motivation, but stays on the surface of conduct. For whatever reason, the original prophet is condemned to death and does indeed die. It all seems grossly unfair. While the evidence is unclear and motives are not revealed, the main point is simple. The prophet had disobeyed. The prophet can only live by obedience. In v. 9 the prophet understood his calling. But now he has begun to relax about it. And his head is turned by an alternative claim. We are given no guidance about sorting out competing claims.

The real point is a simple one: obey God's will. Do not quit on God's will because of royal protest. Do not turn back because of counter advice. Do not be taken in by the generous or the hospitable, nor by those who seem to have a deeper authority. Obedience to God's word is a life and death matter (see Deut 30:15–20). And this prophet—or all Israel—or the church—must attend to that uncompromising mandate. Attend to your call. Hold to it in spite of alternative possibilities. The text offers a radical notion of obedience, unflinching and undaunted by counter proposals.

(a) So a sermon might focus on the radical obedience to which a prophetic church is called. There may be circumstances in which we do not know what the summons is. But not usually. This prophet knew what was expected (vv. 9, 16–17). More often the problem is will and courage rather than more information and guidance. The question to be posed is the nature of obedience and the discernment of what God's will is.

(b) The church is warned not to be bought off from radical obedience, even when it seems authoritative. There are ways of accommodation and ways of faithfulness. As between the two encounters, the text suggests that the greater, more difficult temptation is not political pressure (vv. 6–9) but seductive religion (v. 18).

(c) The death scene (vv. 26–30) is again an oddity. Clearly we are not in the realm of natural death. The death is exceedingly stylized. This is no ordinary or accidental lion, for it has no appetite (v. 28). This is an awesome way in which to speak about the ultimacy of God. Our lives are lived at God's pleasure (see Ezek 18:32) and extend only so far as his good pleasure. This is a harsh God who offers no explanations, but also countenances no vacillation.

(d) One other difficult matter warrants attention. In v. 2 there is an anticipation of Josiah. And in v. 32, there is a future judgment for Bethel. The matter is enigmatic. But this is placed here by the narrators in anticipation of 2 Kings 23:17–19, and looking back to the innovation of 12:29. Our text and 23:17–19 have a promise/fulfillment structure, so that these two texts can only be understood together. Thus the text contains a promise and looks forward. That is a surprise in this text which seems so negative, so preoccupied with death and judgment. I suggest it bespeaks a quite inchoate hope. The narrator presents his case to affirm that God is working out his purposes. He will not quit until he is done (see Phil 1:6). But in the meantime, the bearers of God's way in the world must submit and refuse every friendly accommodation.

The prophetic church faces two dangers. One is a frontal critique from the regime. A subtle but more problematic offer is from like-minded persons. And this latter enigma must be respected in this text. There is something inscrutable here, about which we are not meant to be clear. It is that Israel is not given a context in which obedience is clear and obvious. Rather obedience means clinging desperately to what we do know in the face of all the temptations around us. That means clinging to God's command. But it also means trusting in God's firm intent which will surely have its way (v. 32).

Between the Times (14:1—16:34)

These three chapters form a transition to fill out the chronology. They fill the gap between *the decisive events of chapters 12–13* and *the appearance of Elijah in 17:1*. These chapters are organized around the conventional formulae concerning Kings. Most interesting in them are the several extended narratives.

(1) The king is helpless in the face of the prophet (14:1–20).

(a) The presenting problem is the sickness of the prince. The narrative assumes that the king is helpless. That is, the royal apparatus does not have healing power entrusted to it. Thus the starting point of the narrative is the dysfunctional kingship. Recourse must be made to the prophet who has "all the marbles." What kind of king is it that must go outside social convention to find a healing? It is rather like the medical community sending to Mexico for Laetril. But because of the deep and fundamental hostility of king and prophet, approach for help must be made by an unrecognized "straw party" (vv. 1–3).

(b) Of course the prophet is not fooled by this device, because the prophet functions in concert with the Lord. The Lord is here pro-prophet and anti-king. The narrative thus moves from the sickness of v. 1 to the death of v. 17. The presenting problem of vv. 1–3 and the conclusion of vv. 17–20 belong together. In between we learn why the sickness at the beginning ends in death, and not in life, as we might have expected.

(c) The extended space between (vv. 7–16) is filled with a standard and vigorous prophetic speech. (i) The speech first presents a bill of particulars on the evils of the regime of Jeroboam (vv. 7–9), as though more evidence were needed. The indictment is a disregard of Yahweh and his commandments. In this case, the guilt also includes a rejection of the faith of the Davidic dynasty (v. 8). But of course that is like Catch–22, for to accept that faith (i.e., loyalty to Jerusalem) would mean to cease to being king. (ii) On the basis of such a condemnation, there must be an end to the dynasty (vv. 10–13). The child is incidental and is only a pawn in the larger struggle between Yahweh and this renegade king. (iii) But the indictment goes beyond this brief dynasty to comment on the entire history of North Israel (vv. 15–16). So the narrator has the prophet look far ahead to the disaster of 722 B.C., several dynasties later (see 2 Kings 17:7–41), to see that the entire enterprise must end in exile. And the reason is the enduring one—disregard of Yahweh. We are told in vv. 17–18 that the child died, rather as an omen of what is to come. As the child died, so the dynasty will also. And all this because of the relentless word of God. One can see the same pattern in the south in 2 Sam 12:15b–23, only there it is given a different outcome (vv. 24–25).

(d) This narrative is a summary of the theology of the book of Kings as it concerns the north. The prophetic speech of indictment (vv. 7–9) and the sentence (vv. 10–11) destine Israel to death, without mitigation. The extended narrative to follow traces this sorry tale for 200 years from 922 to 722. But from the beginning, the outcome is clear. It is all hopeless.

This is admittedly remote from an American congregation. But the text makes a point that is not remote. God rules history. God will have his way in spite of governmental mechanization or pseudopiety. God will not be mocked. No close analogy to our time should be drawn because that claims too much. But it is clear that dangerous and unsettling things are happening to America in these last decades of our century. Power is shifting. We have lost our grip in many ways. And it takes no great sensitivity to see that in the midst of this, God is mocked. Perhaps the question for the church concerns a prophetic ministry. That does not mean "righteous indignation" or even social intervention. Rather it means readiness to have the truth spoken which dangerously exposes our systems, not as embodiments of God's will, but as organized forms of mockery and resistance.

(2) The kingship of Judah is duly reported for a period of three kings (1 Kings 14:21—15:24).

(a) Rehoboam (14:21-31) reigned seventeen years. We have already seen his doubtful way in 12:14, so we would not expect anything great. And we are not disappointed. We are told only two things: (i) He was a compromiser on religious matters. Our theologian, looking back to Deut 7:6-11 and 18:9-14, is zealous for the distinctiveness of Israel. Israel is a peculiar people with different loyalties, fears, hopes and norms. Under Rehoboam all of this is disastrously compromised as Judah does "all the abominations of the nations" (v. 24). One might ask now about the "abominations of the nations" in our time which are prohibited to a faithful community. (ii) The Egyptian invasion in 918 (vv. 25-28) is regarded by scholars as historically factual. It is curious that the theologian simply reports this without comment. Unusual for him, he missed a chance to see the invasion as punishment for the affront of vv. 22-24, but the point is not made. In vv. 27-28 we are told of substitute royal instruments of states. When one is compromised as much as is Rehoboam, one is left with only sham forms of power and ersatz instruments of rule. When a society has so violated its dream, it is left with a poor substitute for the real thing.

(b) The regime of Abijam is even less noteworthy (15:1-8). Indeed we are told very little. But Abijam is used by the theologian to insert a theological statement. The dynasty lives only because of the futurities of David. But even these are mixed. On the one hand there is the "Uriah episode" (v. 5, see 2 Sam 11-12) which seems to haunt the Davidic family like Chappiquidick haunts Edward Kennedy. But on the other hand and at the same time, there is the promise to David (2 Sam 7:14-15). The problem for this narrator is the relative power of the *promise* of 2 Sam 7 and the *guilt* of 2 Sam 11-12. Will promise prevail against guilt? Will guilt nullify promise? For now (but not forever) the promise prevails. This is indeed justification by grace. And so a bad king survives because of a promise to the great king. God's immediate judgment is mitigated by his long term commitments to this house. This theologian would have us think about God's long-term commitments which override the demands of the moment (see Matt 28:18–20).

(c) The third Judean king, Asa, is a much more respected leader, one to whom even this hard-nosed historian gives commendation (15:9–14). Asa made massive efforts at fidelity, though even here is a slight qualification (v. 14). It is as though the theologian cannot quite decide how to tilt his report. For in v. 14a there is a "but," in v. 14b there is a "nevertheless." The "nevertheless" prevails. The delicate statement may suggest how close and subjective is our historical reading. It might have tilted that other way with the "but" of v. 14a prevailing. But it does not, not now.

But even this great king could not live outside the real world of political power (vv. 16–25). The narrative is nicely stated. But the brute facts are clear. Asa used the treasures of the temple to buy political and military security from Syria against the near neighbor, Israel. The temple must be sacrificed for survival! Religion has its pragmatic uses. It is curious that this action is not critiqued by the theologian, for it appears to be clearly a compromise of the temple for self-interest. (It is not impossible that the innocent note in v. 23, about sore feet, is a slight castigation. But we are not permitted a judgment more harsh from this characteristically harsh theologian.) We are presented here with a faithful king who did what he had to do to survive. It is clear that even in this architecture of history, not every piece resembles every other. The historian exercises remarkable freedom in selecting data and rendering judgments. Even in this stylized report, historical agents are not interchangeable parts.

(d) No great sweeping conclusion can be drawn on this triad of Rehoboam, Abijam and Asa. Rehoboam is treated as a sorry compromiser; Abijam as the benefactor of the Davidic promise, even though considerable capital from that fund is spent; Asa is a faithful alliance builder. All of them had to live, as faithful people always must, in the tight zone between faithfulness and political realism. This theologian is convinced, however, that political realism is not the last or decisive factor. That role is assigned, even on the horizontal plane of political reality, to the word of Yahweh. This word will have its say, even against the daily darkness. The key issue in these texts is to ask if that has any credence among us. It might be dismissed as an ancient and primitive idea not appropriate to us. Perhaps. But I'll wager the kings thought it irrelevant even in those olden days. So what is it that really powers history? Is it really nothing more than our political scheming for security? These texts shout a loud "no" against that.

(3) The counter-theme of northern kings is less ambiguous and therefore more devastating (15:25—16:34). The north had no government worthy of the name after Jeroboam until Omri. This text recounts the anarchy and hostility among various factors, none of which can claim any legitimacy. The rapid succession might in itself give one pause. Consider, even in our stable democracy, in the brief period of twenty years, 1960–1980, we have had five presidents, one killed in office, one forced out by war, one nearly impeached, two sitting presidents defeated in reelection bids. No close analogy should be drawn. But the text might let this recital ask questions about our own common life. What in fact is at work? Is there a sense to it all? Is there a sense overriding our political non-sense?

(a) Nadab (15:25–32) had the misfortune of being the son of Jeroboam the usurper. The son had to pay for the ways of the father (see Ezek 18:2). Other than a conventional indictment we know nothing. His sin is that he is a northerner. His end, and the end of his dynasty, was already firm in Yahweh's history-shaping word (v. 29, 14:10–16). Kings are helpless in the face of God's overruling way. There are some things beyond the administration of kings. Some national mistakes are paid for, for a long time, even to the third and fourth generations. Nadab has teeth set on edge, precisely for his father's sour grapes.

(b) Baasha is another usurper of which the north has so many (15:33—16:7). Except that this usurper is charged by Yahweh to do what he did (15:29). The overthrow is "according to the word." We know nothing else of Baasha, and indeed his reign is an unimportant episode. But his presentation here is curious and laden with theology. On the one hand, he is "raised up" (*rûm*) by Yahweh (16:2). But immediately, in the very next verse, he is already given a massive sentence of death. In v. 7 we are given another heavy dose of prophetic theology with an odd combination of reasons. Baasha is condemned for destroying the dynasty of Jeroboam, although in 15:29, it seems to have been mandated. And he is condemned for being like the dynasty he replaced. It is as though Yahweh cannot make up his mind. It is like the strange prophetic interchange in 13:11–15, wherein the seducing prophet is used by Yahweh to condemn the first prophet. All these episodes testify to the darkness of history, the shadowy complexity of motivations and the inability to reduce the rawness of history to a single formula or scheme. And the preacher would serve the church well if he/she did nothing more than to help the congregation seriously enter that darkness where we must live and where God's will is being done. The names change. But the realities of faithless dynastic politics persist. And God has no patience with that, even if it is his "legitimate usurper." Both in his rise and in his fall, Baasha's reign is simply a mode of Yahweh's rule. The same God who raises up is the one who brings low. The one who gives life is the one who brings death (see Deut 32:39, 1 Sam 2:6, Isa 45:7). That is true even if the rulers of this age miscalculate and overestimate their own devices.

(c) Elah, son of Baasha, never had a chance (16:8–14). Like Nadab paid for his father Jeroboam (15:25–31), so Elah must pay for his father Baasha. The measure of Elah's incompetence and insecurity is that, upon enthronement, he killed all potential rivals in the royal family (v. 11). His demise is sealed already in v. 3, simply implemented in v. 12 by Zimri, another usurper who fulfills the prophetic word. The narrative portrays a sordid hopelessness which cannot endure in the face of God's governance. There is an "utter sweeping away" and no royal agent can resist the purpose of God.

(d) Zimri was a military commander who tried a coup (16:15–20), who hardly reckons as a king. He apparently had little following, for "all Israel" immediately turned away from him (v. 16). His cause hopeless, he ended in suicide. He is the "conspirator" par excellence. His name appears to have become a slogan as the "Benedict Arnold" of legitimate rule (see 2 Kings 9:31). He is, even for this harsh critic of kings, the quintessence of illegitimacy.

(e) Since the death of Jeroboam, Israel has been waiting

for Omri (16:21–28), like France waiting for DeGaulle. He is the first stable leader since that time, the interim period characterized by disorder and disarray. In three ways Omri is like David:

(i) He is regarded in the ancient Near East as a powerful leader. He had a good reputation. Long after his death and that of his dynasty, Israel is referred to in non-biblical documents as "the house of Omri." He seems to have had the force to bring order and the appearance of legitimacy to his people. The yearning for legitimacy is worth reflecting on.

(ii) He also purchased his own city for his capitol. Like Jerusalem became "David's city" (2 Chron 12:16, 21:1), free from Israelite tradition, so Omri's Samaria is his private turf. Like David, Omri had a vision of personal power. Sociological analysis makes clear that such private cities were the locus of self-serving power and inevitably practiced exploitative economics against the peasants who paid the taxes. Such a city surely works against the solidarity of the tribal structure.

(iii) Like David, Omri begat a prominent son who was to be a great king, an enormous syncretizer and a notorious exploiter of people.

Likely the preachable point in Omri is the contrasting judgments made on him by his political contemporaries (in non-biblical texts) who relish his greatness, and the Bible which regards him as the nadir of faithlessness. We have no way to assess these different evaluations, except that we are now seeking to understand and practice a biblical view of history. In that context the judgments of the world must be dismissed for the sake of another reading of reality (see 1 Sam 16:7, 2 Cor 5:16). The point is that the Bible does not proceed by the ways of the world. And, we might ask, how are we discerned, given the criteria of biblical faith?

(f) Finally in this pitiful narrative, we come to Ahab, Omri's son (16:29–34). We know from other sources that Ahab was one of Israel's great leaders. But the treatment here is like the pall placed over the casket at the funeral of a great, dead man. Now he looks like all the others. He is not more important. The narrator has a way of reducing such greatness to proportion in the context of God's governing word. The theological formulae of this historian serve as a leveler, to dismiss the greatness here judged not great. This historian is just not interested in the norms of the world. Judged by these peculiar criteria, Ahab is another spectacular failure. In addition to the stereotyped formula, he did two specific, interrelated things which bring harsh judgment. One, he intermarried with the Phoenicians by taking the princess Jezebel for his wife (shades of Solomon; see 1 Kings 3:1, 11:1). Indeed the whole episode sounds like a replay of Solomon. Two, and derivatively, he built a cult for the gods of Jezebel (see 1 Kings 11:4–5). He is judged by our writer the very worst (v. 33), for he compromised everything that was important to Israel. Israel is characterized and authorized by adherence to the first commandment, exclusive zeal for Yahweh. And when that is compromised, as it is so blatantly here, everything is at risk. Since 1 Kings 13, everything in our narrative has been building toward this moment. Now the narrator takes a deep breath and moves to Elijah in 17:1: "Now Elijah. . . ." The historian will spend a long time on Ahab, because Elijah must needs receive extensive coverage. The history of Israel is the history of the first commandment and its violation (see 18:18, 21; 19:10). Ahab is of little zeal, and so history must break apart for him. Contrast the zeal of Elijah (19:10, 14). (The special note of v. 34 is enigmatic, but relates in some way to Josh 6:26. It may reflect the low morality and syncretism of this monarchy which tries to secure the well-being of a new city with a child sacrifice. It may also show the ambition of Ahab in rebuilding an old city, with the nerve even to violate an old curse. Could it mean that Ahab is so throughly secularized that he is not deterred by any such religious fear or tabu? Perhaps Ahab's action suggests that if there is no god, everything is possible.)

Thus the narrative moves quickly through six northern kings. It is a tale of unrelieved disaster. It features the collapse of two quick dynasties, one brief coup which failed and the rise of a strong dynasty which, from its inception, is condemned for syncretism. The historian builds his case slowly but firmly. The whole recital points to the end of the north in 2 Kings 17:7–41. The issue is why has all failed. In contrast to God's promise which does not fail (Josh 21:43–45), every royal, human effort at well-being does fail. The answer to the question is in 17:13–14: all has failed because the prophets were ignored. Where the prophets are ignored, where Yahweh is denied, where his commandments are nullified, there can only come trouble. The kings seek to be autonomous, self-reliant, depending on other resources, religious and political. But the historian knows better. There are no alternatives to the rule of Yahweh. There is only this single rule of history. All the others are counterfeits. Well-being, public and personal, depends on listening (obeying). That *history* should be understood as *obedience* is of course very strange to us. And it is not easy to preach in a culture which imagines itself to be self-invented. And preachers are left here with two very hard questions:

(1) How can we understand this mode of reality, even to think in terms of obedience?

(2) How could we specify the substance of history as obedience? If we were to obey, what would we do?

So the theologian who gives us these texts would drive us back to the torah which is also the memory to which Jesus pressed his people (Matt 5:17–20; 23:23; Mark 7:1–13; 10:17–22).

God-Ordained "Trouble"
(1 Kings 17:1—22:53)

These chapters constitute some of the most poignant theological material in the Old Testament and some of the richest possibilities for preaching. At 1 Kings 17:1 it is clear that the normal royal recital breaks off. We are offered a quite alternative literature which intrudes on the rather symmetrical narrative. In these chapters (and well into 2 Kings), we have stories about prophets. Indeed a significant percentage of *"Kings"* is in fact a presentation of *"prophets."* And that in itself is an important consideration for preaching. It suggests that the texts are not overly impressed with kings and in fact do not believe the kings are the real makers of Israel's history. Rather the kings are incidental public points of reference which simply provide a context for the real history-makers, who are the prophets. At the most, the kings may be convenient for school children to memorize and for the making of time-lines. But they do not matter decisively for understanding the narrative or the events it reports. According to this presentation, the prophets are the real "makers of history." They bring the overriding purpose of God to bear upon events. And that is what makes the sequence of events as important as it is.

These texts are not heavily influenced by Deuteronomic theology, as are other parts of the books of Kings. They seem to be early tales, left in their primary form, preserved by people who valued the prophets, who believed that in remembering the prophets, they were being faithful. This means that the texts are highly dramatic and operate with a highly imaginative style. Characteristically they offer a new reality to the hearer, a mode of life that does not yield to or compromise with the royal claims. Thus they serve to articulate an alternative way of living and an alternative way of knowing. So the preacher might press to ask folks *how* they know what they know. Whom do we believe?

In effect these tales serve rhetorically to delegitimate the kings, to dismiss the entire royal perception of reality. That is, they assert that the world is not the way the kings say it is. The kings perceive a false world. Kings may just be *mistaken* or they may be *lying* to protect their skewed interests.

When these same stories are later used by the Deuteronomic historian in the exile, they seem to suggest a connection between *royal ways* and *exile*. That is, the reason Israel is in exile is because it followed royal ways and believed "royal truths." And the clear intent of the material is to affirm that the way out of exile is to quit thinking like a king and embrace the alternative world dramatized by the prophets. Thus the material is a *call to repentance* about basic suppositions. In preaching from these texts, the preacher will discover that the only way for the text to have its full say is if the pastor and the congregation really intend to engage the dangerous possibility of thinking an alternative thought and characterizing an alternative world. The new world given in these texts is a world in which God's way and God's word have their decisive influence. The intent of these texts is not to invite us to be irrational. But the texts do reject the rationality of the king and invite Israel (and us) to a different, subversive rationality.

The Initial Appearance of Elijah (17:1–24)

Elijah appears abruptly. That is how God's word comes into the royal arena, and into the royal narrative. Like King Ahab, we are scarcely prepared for Elijah. His name means "Yahweh is my God." It is a buoyant confession of faith, surely abrasive, for it means to deny the claims of other gods. His very presence in the text raises the God question for us: whom do you trust?

The situation in these episodes is an energy crisis—no rain. The king, whose business is economic well-being (fertility) cannot cause rain to fall. There is only one implication: he is an incompetent, ineffective king. The announcement of the drought means to delegitimate the king. (What have you done for us lately?) But we are told another thing: rain is not given, not because of the king's failure, but because Yahweh will be God. So the drought is a pointer between the rival claims of a king who cannot make rain and a God who can give or withhold well-being. The preacher must not be detained by speculative questions about the cause of rain. It is enough to hear the claim of the text on its own terms.

It will be sufficient to stay with the text, to be invited to a simple, uncritical *amazement*—wonder that things are not and do not have to be the way the king said they were. Thus the stories are subversive. They hint of a way around royal administration. And that way concerns the transcendent power of God which always surprises us.

In this narrative, Elijah appears before the king in two episodes before the text moves on to more weighty matters:

(1) In 17:1–7 Elijah is a man under *a word*. He knows he must do things, compelled by God's command, even though it seems *a little foolish*. So a sermon might be offered on the foolishness of God which empowers people to do scandalous things for the sake of God's purposes (see 1 Cor 1:25, 4:10). Think about what the world regards as "foolish," which might yield the peace, mercy and justice which God wills.

(a) Elijah is commanded to be fed by ravens, and to drink only from the brook. He is to shun all the regular supplies of food (see Dan 1:8; Mark 8:15) which are guaranteed by conventional administration. He is to become utterly vulnerable and rely only on what God gives (see Matt 6:25–33). The command of God sends people into high risk.

(b) The command of God is shown to be utterly reliable. The ravens did as the heavenly Father promised. The brook did provide water, not forever but until the promise had been kept. God's promises are sure and can be trusted. The text offers a juxtaposition of *human vulnerability* and *divine power*. Perhaps promises are only kept to vulnerable people (see Mark 8:35). Certainly king Ahab who resisted being vulnerable never knew any promises from God.

(c) This text invites the church to remember ancient times, clear back to the miracle of manna (Exod 16). That old story is now reenacted. And in the same way, the text rushes toward Jesus and the new way in which we are invited to pray (Matt 6:11). Like the disciples, the prophet prays daily for bread.

(d) Obviously, such a scene will seem remote to modern people. But the preacher must take care not to be too relevant. I do not believe the call of the text is to go out and "trust the birds." Rather, it is an invitation to become vulnerable in the way Jesus risked his person. The scene asks us to identify the deep safeguards of conventional order and sustenance we are called to give up. Where is the wild territory we are called to enter for the sake of the gospel? The text affirms that when God is obeyed enough to risk such dangers, surprising gifts are given. Correspondingly, God's gifts are not given or seen among those who have everything guaranteed (see Mark 6:1–6).

(2) The other introductory episode of 17:8–24 puts the prophet in juxtaposition with a foreign widow. His partner in this story is important. First, she is a nobody—a widow, who in that society had no standing, worth or significance. Second, she was not even an Israelite, but a foreigner. God's command sends his faithful prophet for nourishment outside all the predictable places of well-being. Note that Jesus introduces the scandal of the gospel by reference to this command (Luke 4:25–26).

(a) The theme of vulnerability is continued. Elijah is not sent to *help*, but to *be fed*, not to give, but to receive. Elijah is sent by the Lord to submit to this Gentile widow, to depend on the gifts and resources of this nobody. There is an abrupt reversal of roles. The one whom we expect to be strong is needful and must submit to the wretched of the earth. The episode is paralleled in the story of Jesus at the well (John 4:1–7). Jesus also does not *give* water but first *asks* for a drink. With both Elijah and Jesus, they emerge the strong helper, but only after they have submitted as the one in need. *Strength* seems to come by way of *needfulness*.

(b) The prophet intervenes in the life of the widow (vv. 13–16). The *bearer of God's Word* engages one of *the worthless ones*. He might have done more grandiose things. But he does not. There is a special linkage in the Bible between *the caring word* and *the worthless*. And the connection is made by obedience.

(c) The prophet intervenes with a powerful word, "Do not fear." That is the primal intrusion of the Gospel. This word authoritatively spoken creates a new situation. And the situation-shattering word is matched by a deed of plenty. Where this powerful man is present, there is enough to eat. The prophet could do what the king could not do. The calculating economic program of the king kept poor people poor.

The breaking of the endless cycle of need and poverty is broken by the intervention of God. The prophetic ministry to which Elijah is called shatters the tired world of hopelessness. And the point of preaching is to affirm that such deeply obedient risk-taking, speech-bearing folks can function to make the world new. It is the deception of the king to make us believe the world is fixed and must stay the drought-ridden way it is. The king wants people to be and stay hopeless, because hopeless people will never challenge. That shell of hopelessness is now broken by a concrete act of powerful compassion.

(d) Now in v. 17, the stakes are upped. Now it is not merely hunger but *death*. Now the prophet must face the "last enemy" (1 Cor 15:20). Death in the case of this young man is having its way. But the prophet, bearer of God's word, engages death. The scenario is prayer and by physical action. The outcome is LIFE.

This episode of course looks toward the same action by Jesus (Mark 5:35–43). Now at one level we can reflect on a dead child and the raising. That is what the text says. But as the text is now used, neither with Elijah nor Jesus is there an interest in death as such. In both cases, the interest is on the *authority of the life-bringer*. So they are angered with Jesus (Mark 5:13, 6:2). With Elijah the woman confesses his authority. That is what we are to face. A flat, administered world of talk-shows and opinion polls has the result of reducing everything to hopeless predictability and normalcy. That same thing was done in the time of Elijah, and not by happenstance. Kings want to eliminate prophets because they are too inconvenient.

(e) Well, says the text, life is inconvenient. It cannot be controlled or administered or predicted. It breaks out in ways that offend. And that is where God's holy word works. The preacher must not back off from the radical claim of this text. It is that life comes by God's word in the midst of death. But we must not permit the text to be relegated to either a world of magic, nor to the "end time." Folks can be helped to focus on the *daily season of death* that besets us, in the face of fear, grief, guilt, hate, fascination with self. Along with king Ahab, we draw more and more into a closed, self-preoccupied world. And it is killing. Now comes the one who can break it open. As with the widow mother, we are stunned when it happens. What the text knows is that God's power for life is still at work in the hopeless, closed contexts of our daily round. It is still at work in concrete ways through called, authorized human agents.

Meeting the King, Discerning the Real King (18:1–46)

Chapter 17 is like the preliminary match. It is staged to have something to do while the crowd gathers. Eventually we get to the main match. The prophet must face the king. Who could have known it would be such a mismatch? Facing the king in chapter 18 is more formidable than facing the alien widow in 17. When the prophet meets the king, two worlds collide. Two views of reality conflict. It is like Amos before Amaziah (Amos 7:10–17), like Jesus before Pilate (John 18:28—19:16). And always the two of them discuss the same question: "What's true" (John 18:38)? The king has his notion of truth—only it does not hold, and eventually even the king does not believe it. But the king can hardly consider a real truth, for the real truth will undermine his view of the world and delegitimate his authority. The task of the preacher here may be to join the issue, to see that always we stand between the gospel and the "royal truth" which seduces us. Pilate's question is still a live question. What really can we count on, for "truth" means "reliable." We have grown careless about believing too much and trusting too easily, finding out too late that what we believe is in fact nonsense. So the question of the text may be: who gets to decide what is true and reliable?

(1) The meeting with the king is a dramatic movement of scenes, carefully prepared for. The narrative moves from the initial *command of v. 1* to the amazing *resolution of vv. 41–46*. Preaching on this narrative should enable the congregation to move dramatically from the command to the rain. Along the way, the congregation becomes aware of the alternative resolution which is tried and rejected. Questions may be, what are the issues that need to be resolved for us, i.e., what form does the drought take? What are the alternative resolu-

tions we trust in? What would it mean to have life resolved on the terms of this radical God who can make all things new?

(a) The context for the issue of truth (reliability) is the drought (vv. 1–2). And from drought there is famine. The context is the failure of the king. The king is the principle of reliability, for if the king can't deliver, who can? The king is the source of life, but the animals are already dying. So from the beginning the king is on the defensive, put there by God's decree (about which he does not know) that there be a drought. The regime is not working. As nature wanes, the government is in jeopardy. The question of truth comes to surface because conventional truth is in jeopardy. Nobody really believes the royal truth. Nobody really expects it to "work." The preacher might help the congregation to see that this is in fact our situation as well. The "old truths" have failed. "Ancient Good" is more than "uncouth." It has failed.

(b) This is subversive literature, designed to unmask the king. So it pauses to engage in a little sarcastic humor. The king is presented in a ludicrous light (vv. 3–6). He should have been forming policy, engaging in high government business. But instead he is hunting grass for the animals. It is as though he is not really king any more—and he knows it! The power of the "truth" has a way of dethroning false kings and putting an end to their claims. That is what Pharaoh discerned in the Exodus, Nebuchadnezzar in the book of Daniel, and Herod and Pilate in the gospels. False claims cannot hold in the face of reality. So the king is set up in this narrative for failure. The monarchy is a charade of feebleness.

(c) After the preliminary meeting with Obadiah (vv. 7–16), the meeting with the king in vv. 17–19 is dramatic. The preacher can pose the question: who indeed is the trouble-maker in this story (cf. v. 17)? And what is the real trouble? From the first instant, the prophet is labeled "trouble-maker." That is predictable. The one who speaks the truth is a trouble-maker, a carpetbagger, a communist or whatever. Who do we mark as trouble-makers? And why? What had he done to cause trouble? So far as we are told, he had only (a) made himself *vulnerable* (17:1–7), (b) valued the foreign *widow* (17:8–16) and (c) introduced *life* into a closed world of death (17:17-24). But perhaps that is enough. The king finds such interventions intolerable. He does not want able people to be *vulnerable*. He does not want *widows* to be valued, especially foreigners. He certainly does not want *life* brought into his safe, closed world of death. One might think it all rather innocuous, or even welcome. But the king knew better. The live word of God is a threat and a trouble to Ahab's false government. And it is even more so when concretely enacted by such an abrasive person. So we might consider the fraudulent loyalties we nurture, in spite of the data. We may find the emergence of holy words and new life too dangerous. So we can most easily dismiss it with a label: troubler, traitor, communist!

The prophet of course does not flinch. He turns the tables. He returns the label. He dares to say that the king himself is the real troubler. The king is the traitor. The king is rejected because he holds to a way of rule which rejects the power of God. Note Hos 4:6: "...because you have rejected knowledge, I reject you from being a priest to me." One rejection begets another. Every practice of authority is thereby called into question, in family, in church, in community. Authority which seeks to fence out the purpose of God for life is finally a troubler. And soon or late, the live word has its say against such authority.

(2) But the confrontation with the king is preliminary. It only sets the issue. We must not be too impressed with such meetings with the king, for *the real meeting concerns the Hidden One* who stands apart from and over against every king. This dramatic meeting is cast in two parts, negative and positive, and the interaction of the two parts intensifies the suspense.

(a) The issue is sharply posed (vv. 20-21). The real human problem is our "limp," not deciding, refusing to choose, wanting to have it both ways. Accommodation displaces commitment. Jesus understood that one cannot serve two masters (Matt 6:24), but we keep trying and hoping. We will not choose because the loyalties that seduce us seem to give too much (see Hos 2:8). And the true God seems not to give so much, so we put off the choice.

(b) The negative element of this meeting (vv. 22-29) is a carefully crafted taunting dismissal of the "no-gods" (see

Deut 32:21). The gods are put on trial. They are given every chance. But the narrative is bold and relentless, for it knows. And the conclusion is like a rhetorical twisting of the knife of ridicule, to make the point, to make the pain and humiliation last longer: "no voice—no one answered—no one heeded." Baal is one big zero!

(c) The positive counterpart is a sharp contrast (vv. 30–35). Yahweh is shown to be the one who makes and keeps promises. The rhetorical function is to lead the listening congregation through the narrative experience of waiting and trusting, perhaps waiting too long and trusting too much, and beginning to wonder. And then to be surprised by the good news! Here we have a narrative interlude which heightens the tension and makes the context more rigorous for Yahweh and more vivid for Israel. This is no set-up. Yahweh will have to act decisively.

(d) The prayer and response of vv. 36–40 is closely structured. First, Elijah is a man of prayer, not magic. He does not manipulate but waits for a gift. Elijah is a receiver, not an agent. His address to God is a lordly one, three times naming the name of the exodus God (vv. 31–37). Second, the answer from God is abrupt and terse (v. 38). It is almost lost in the narrative. In this one inexplicable turn the entire narrative is broken open. The One for whom Israel waited has come. Everything is changed. The decisive yet modest assertion here is not unlike the narrative of the birth of Isaac in Gen 21:1–7. After all this wait, one almost misses the turn wrought by God. Third, the response of "the nations" is a glad acknowledgment of the true God (vv. 39–40). There is no explanation, nor is there embarrassment. Our faith relies on a story. It must be told and left to make its own case. Our lives are intruded upon, we know not how (see John 9:25). The New Testament stories of Jesus are about such intrusions that make things new. The preacher must leave the text in its abrasiveness, incongruous with our usual expectations and our conventional ways of knowing.

(3) *The end of the narrative* in vv. 41–46 looks back to the drought of vv. 1–2. Things are resolved here. Because of Yahweh's intervention, there is an end to the limp. Israel no longer shrinks, but is able to trust. The show of power in the fire (v. 38) is only an anticipation of the real life-giving of rain here. What can one do with a fire? It is only an exhibi-

tion. And if that is all, then it does not matter. But now there is rain and that changes life in the earth. The narrator enjoys this last part of the story because now the tables are turned. Now king Ahab is completely at the disposal of Elijah. He could not cope with the drought. He can only wait now with all the other needful ones. He has been dramatically dethroned, to make way for the real God who gives life. Elijah now holds all the cards. Ahab is a frail suppliant at best. The king has been displaced. That always happens where the true life-giving God becomes visible. The purpose of the narrative, when it was told and each time it is retold, is to make the life-giving God visible.

A Wanted Man! (19:1–21)

Elijah is a wanted man! He had acted according to his prophetic mandate. And like always, that got him in a lot of trouble. The result of his action was subversive. The preacher can use this narrative about this dangerous man to evidence the subversive quality of prophetic faith, whenever it is embraced.

(1) *Elijah is wanted by the queen* (vv. 1–3). Jezebel is not a "nice lady," but a ruthless politician who will protect her interests in whatever way necessary. And because she is not "nice," Elijah is not safe. He is an enemy of the state. For the sake of his life, he heads to the wilderness, south to Beer-Sheba. Beer-sheba is the jumping-off place, the wild region beyond effective royal control. The "wilderness" which escapes the dominant rationality is often a place for sanctuary (see Luke 3:2). He headed for the border.

(2) Elijah may be wanted by the state. But *he does not want himself.* He does not value his own life (vv. 4–8). This little paragraph is transition between his confrontation with the queen (vv. 1–3) and his confrontation with the real king (Yahweh; vv. 9–18). This section can be structured in two ways.

(a) Taken by itself it is structured in the exchange between a depressed, hopeless man and a responding, ministering angel. The speech of Elijah (v. 4) is a lament, even a death-wish. The text might be preachable to "burned out liberals." He has taken his mission seriously, so seriously that he is isolated and has no courage to go on any more. The response of the angel (vv. 5–7) counters that wish and offers a "life-wish" against his death-wish. Burdened by an impossible mission, Elijah does not have within him resources for life. But those resources are given in the flow of the narrative. They are given unexpectedly, inexplicably—just given. There is an evangelical abruptness about the gift, an angel where there seemed to be only brooding death. The coming of the angel is not unlike the angel to rejected Hagar (Gen 15:7–10, 21:16–19). One may reflect on the concrete life-restoring function of food, the most elemental sign of caring (see 2 Sam 16:27–29; Mark 6:30–42). It is such a simple thing as "cake and water" which is the effective sign of God's presence. The narrative, indeed, Elijah's life, at this point, becomes an affirmation of a new future. But it is because of the angel least expected. Without the angel, the story would leave us with a hopeless fugitive.

(b) Or one can pursue this encounter in terms of the incongruity between vv. 1–3 and vv. 4–8, a play on the word "life" (nephesh). In v. 2, the queen wants his life. In v. 3, he flees for his life. And yet in v. 4 he despairs his life and wants to abandon it. The interplay of vv. 2–3 and v. 4 is a discerning one. The same one despairs his life and yet does not want it taken from him. Elijah wants to die, but he fears to be killed. Or perchance he is simply offering hyperbole which he does not really mean. Maybe he is depressed but means something less than death. In any case, the angel response takes life seriously, will not give him over to death, even when he chooses it. Thus the angel ministers. But the angel also resists. The angel will not give Elijah over to the death he wishes. Because God has other fish for Elijah yet to fry.

(3) Elijah is wanted by God (vv. 9–18). He is wanted more passionately by God than even by Jezebel. The dangerous encounter with Jezebel pales before this awesome meeting. In chapter 18, Elijah was the conspicuous champion of Yahweh. But here he appears to get more than he bargains for. The presentation of this encounter at Horeb is an "instant replay" of Moses at Horeb. The claim of the narrative may be that this generation also has its theological "heavy." And so this generation also is held in Yahweh's demanding covenant. The narrative is presented in two moves which are closely paralleled. I do not find the repetition an intrusion, but simply a way to extend the story in its tension.

(a) In vv. 9–13a, there is a first exchange:

(i) God asks about Elijah's purpose (v. 9). That is the nature of the relation. Elijah must give answer for himself. Yahweh has a lordly right to ask.

(ii) Elijah answers by telling how faithful he has been, how many risks he has taken, and how much his life is threatened (v. 10). The response is self-serving. One would imagine he came to Horeb simply to celebrate his personal faithfulness. Note that again in v. 10, he refers to the life crisis of vv. 2–3. He states the unbearable contrast between the overriding *commitment* of his life and the deep *danger* to his life.

(iii) In vv. 11–13a, Yahweh graciously makes himself available, gives himself to this one whose life has been "wasted." This is a famous passage giving special nuance to the way of God's presence. But not too much should be made of the famous "still small voice." John Gray suggestively renders it, "a sound of thin silence." Samuel Terrien has it, "the sound of utmost silence" which can be "cut with a knife." This is not the voice of conscience but of *awe*, not romantic whisperings but overriding *majesty*. God's inscrutable holiness is not packaged in utilitarian ways. For all his graciousness, God stays free of any grasping Elijah may want to do of him. In this drastic moment, Elijah becomes freshly aware that it is Yahweh and none other and not himself, who is God. All his fears are set in proper place. There is now only one to fear, the same one who must be obeyed.

(b) The second series of exchanges is structured like the first (vv. 13b–18). It is partly a repetition, partly an advance, surely heightening the dramatic tension. The first exchange (vv. 9–13a) was noticeably enigmatic. Now the second exchange becomes concrete and clear:

(i) Again it begins with the same lordly question (v. 13b), as though God seeks a better answer than was given the first time.

(ii) Elijah's response is the same (v. 14). He decides not to change his story, even if it is self-serving. It is again self-serving, alluding back to the threat of Jezebel and his own utter fidelity.

(iii) But the third element is new (vv. 15–18). Elijah is wanted by Yahweh for a very particular reason. That is why the preacher must not linger on the theophany or the "still small voice." Here all that "religion business" is moved to *subversive mission* in the world. God's appearance is never an end in itself, but that the world should be transformed.

So the one who had sought *safety* is set on a new mission of *danger*. The encounter moves the agenda from the despair and fear of Elijah, to the dreams of Yahweh. Now Elijah is to instigate a two-fold political coup and secure his own successor. All of this he does not do, but the demand lingers over the rest of this prophetic tale, in the following chapters. His new mandate contains some irony. He was done in by his earlier confrontation with Jezebel. But that is as nothing compared with this. The stakes are now considerably upped. Now he must move to the big league (see Jer 12:5).

And then in v. 18, there is the inclusion of a marvelous footnote by Yahweh: "Oh, by the way. . . ." Elijah has it wrong. He had miscalculated. He had thought he was the only one (vv. 10, 14) taking himself much too seriously. He had miscounted by 6,999. The situation of Yahweh's future is not that hopeless. So Elijah can take heart. But as he does that, he always must take himself not quite so seriously. He can now see himself in perspective. There are 7000 that he can count on, even as God counts on them. There is anticipated here a faithful community that withstands every syncretistic seduction. And Elijah can draw courage for his own mandate.

(4) Vv. 19–21 are something of addendum or a transition. They show the narrator looking ahead with a concern for the continuity of the prophets and the well-being of the next generation (see 2 Kings 2:1–12). Here one might reflect on the character of the prophetic call:

(a) It is mediated through a human agent. Elisha is not called in an isolated, mystical experience, but he is designated by a named, known person.

(b) The call is radical and uncompromising. There is no bargaining or resisting. Elisha is claimed! He knows it and he must follow.

(c) The call requires a radical break with his old arrangements. The call is a departure (see Gen 12:1–3; Mark 10:17–22). But unlike Jesus (see Matt 8:21–17; Luke 9:61), Elisha is permitted a chance to get his house in order.

The movement of the entire passage is telling. It begins with Elijah in danger, down and depressed. He is fearful, under assault and unsure. By the end, he is not only restored and buoyant, prepared to move on. He is even willing to be a recruitment officer for the future of the movement. The preacher may let this text be a narrative experience of the move from *exhausted disarray* to *new energy* for the faithful. The move made in this narrative toward new faithfulness is accomplished by:

    (a) withdrawal with articulated depression
    (b) surprised nourishment from an unexpected angel
    (c) confrontation with the holy One, not to be packaged for usefulness
    (d) articulation of a fresh, dangerous task
    (e) refutation of a false self-perception
    (f) renewal with a new assistant.

By the end, the one who was *wanted by the kingdom*, then *wanted more urgently by God*, also now wants to get on with it.

Royal Strategies, Prophetic Intrusions (20:1–43)

All during the ninth century, the kingdom of Syria was a concern of Israel. It was variously partner, ally, threat, master, servant. The present chapter reflects on the delicacy and danger of that complex relationship. The chapter appears to be a misfit in the extended narrative cluster about the prophets, for this one is oddly about kings and wars. But closer review indicates that this chapter also is in fact a "prophetic narrative," for prophets take the decisive roles in vv. 13, 22, 28. Worth noting is the fact that both the prophet and the "man of God" are nameless figures, suggesting it was their *word* and not their *persons* which concerns us.

(1) In the beginning of the narrative, Syria under Ben-Hadad has the upper hand (vv. 1–12). He makes heavy economic demands on Israel as "protection money." At first, Ahab the king agrees (vv. 1–6). But in governmental consultation, the king is advised not to concede so much (vv. 7–8). In this case the government is more hawkish than the king and is willing to risk confrontation rather than to concede too much.

In the final part of the preliminary negotiation, there is a movement toward inevitable war. Ben-Hadad asked too much. Israel will not grant so much. The nations posture and are soon at the brink. In the response of Ahab (v. 9), there is

some uncertainty, because the difference between "first demand" and "this thing" is not clear. Presumably the difference is between delivery of payment (v. 3) and a more
general and comprehensive search and plunder (v. 6). While
the former is acceptable, the latter is an unthinkable affront.
So there is saber-rattling on both sides (vv. 10–11). Negotiation is escalated to conflict. But the interpreter must not linger here, for this is only stage-setting.

(2) The middle portion of the narrative (vv. 13–30a) concerns us more directly because it is the point of *prophetic intervention* and because it is the place of *radical inversion*. The
first encounter of war is instigated by a prophet (vv. 13–21).
In vv. 1–12, one has the impression that Israel is the lesser
party. But against these generally recognized odds, the
prophet urges confrontation and promises victory.

(a) The conversation between prophet and king is crucial
(vv. 13–14). In the prophetic speech, everything is settled.
And the key element is the prophetic assertion, "You shall
know I am Yahweh" (v. 13). This formula occurs often in the
Old Testament. Walther Zimmerli has urged that it is this
war context of I Kings 20 which is the foundational usage
from which the other uses derive. Israel's God is known as
the one who intervenes to cause victories and invert situations. Indeed the revelations of God in the Bible are characteristically inverting interventions. And that claim runs from
the Exodus through the ministry of Jesus even to the resurrection. God's disclosures are victories surprisingly given
against unbelievable odds.

(b) The battle is joined according to the strategem of the
prophet (vv. 15–21). Israel is successful. The prophet is vindi-
cated. Yahweh is shown to be decisive.

(3) Vv. 22–25 provide an interlude between battles.
Again the prophet appears (v. 22), urging military preparation. The general strategy of Syria is presented in vv. 23–25.
It is premised in the recognition that Israel is a guerilla people who live and fight in the hill country. That is, they are
poor people who do not have all the "rational" means of war
possessed by Syria. Syria simply proposes to fight where it
has the advantage. But along with a political strategem, a
theological judgment is made. Yahweh is thought by Syria to
be simply an appendage of Israel. Yahweh is here nothing
more than the weakness and strength of Israel writ large.

Syria does not suggest that Yahweh has his own life, free of
Israel. Thus in the mouth of the Syrian, religion is only code
language for military prowess. The same opinion of God is
reflected in Stalin's cynical question, "How many divisions
does the Pope have?" Is there nothing more to faith than political realism?

(4) The issue is joined in vv. 25–30a. Again the crucial
role is played not by kings and commanders, but by the man
of God.

(a) The crucial element is the prophetic statement of v.
28. In a direct refutation of bad Syrian religion, Yahweh's
victory is said to be a demonstration that he is not a mere
appendage of political and military power. The Syrians had
badly miscalculated if they thought Yahweh was limited to
Israel's military equipment. Yahweh is capable of free, sovereign action over and against the nations. Yahweh clearly has
distance and transcendence over Israel. A sermon might be
offered on the freedom of God apart from God's patron
people.

(b) In v. 28 the formula of victory-disclosure is again
used (see v. 13). Yahweh is known to be sovereign. There is no
other explanation for the unexpected victory. Thus Syria is
refuted in its wrong theological notion. As a result, Israel's
hill country definition is shattered. And Yahweh is disclosed
as free Lord. The enemy is routed (vv. 29–30a, see Exod
14:30–31).

(5) In the penultimate scene (vv. 30b–34), the situation is
reversed. Now Ben Hadad is the suppliant. Now Ahab is in
the power position. The end result is a treaty between them
(v. 34), but the terms are completely favorable to Ahab. There
has been a role reversal from vv. 1–21.

Thus the structure of the passage makes the main point:

at the beginning:	The inversion	at the end:
vv. 1–12	vv. 13–30a	vv. 30b–34
Syria dominates		Israel dominates
Israel	prophetic intervention	Syria
	vv. 13, 22, 28	

The decisive element is the prophetic *intervention* which
causes the *inversion*. Of these three interventions, the second

is incidental. The decisive ones are the first (v. 13) and the
third (v. 28). Both use the formula of disclosure. The entire
narrative shows that *the humble (Ahab–Israel) is exalted*, and
the exalted (Ben-Hadad–Syria) is humbled. And this change of
status is caused by prophetic speech. There is, to be sure, real
war, real scheming and real suffering. But all of that is ener-
gized by faith in and word from this God who will be confined by no theological reduction, either of Israel (who
expects nothing) or of Syria (who categories God). The story
is focused on the character of this God who breaks all the
categories and shows himself to be a free agent in the world.
Such a claim is remote from the consciousness of most modern people. And so it is likely that the narrative form itself is
our best mode of proclamation.

(6) The last scene in this narrative is a strange one (vv.
35–43). It may be an addendum to the story, for the preceding account appears complete and symmetrical, ending at v.
34. Again, in this scene, the action concerns a prophet, one
who regularly claims initiative with the king.

(a) The prophet wishes to give the appearance of a
wounded warrior (vv. 35–36). While the king is always serious, doing rational business, the prophet must penetrate that
inordinate seriousness. To do so, every ploy can be used, including a disguise. So the prophet seeks to create a new reality which outflanks the sobriety of the king. In this
preliminary comment, it is dangerous business not to obey a
prophet, even if the command seems absurd.

(b) In vv. 37–40, we have an acted parable, an exchange
which turns out to be a ploy. But the king does not know it.
Kings are dangerous people to confront head-on. So like Nathan in 2 Sam 12:1–7, the prophet enacts a scene designed to
have the king indict himself. In this sense of make-believe,
the "man who escaped" is nameless and unimportant. But
the point is established. A soldier under orders cannot permit
a captive to escape, on pain of death. The king need not even
pronounce the verdict. It is perfectly obvious.

(c) Thus in vv. 41–43, the exchange is disclosed as street
theatre. The real life situation of vv. 41–43 is illuminated by
the playlet of vv. 37–40, in which the king did not know he
was a participant. Only now the king is the man under judgment (self-pronounced), for letting one escape. And the one

who unfortunately escaped is Ben-Hadad. The king stands
under judgment. No wonder he went home sullen, under sentence of death which he himself expressed in v. 40.

The narrative takes a curious turn. In v. 34, Ben-Hadad
had conceded everything. And in response Ahab had made a
new favorable treaty. But he had let him live! Or better, he
had let him escape. To Ahab, this must have been good practical politics. But to the prophet, this practice of politics was
bad theology, for Ben-Hadad had been given over to be destroyed. Prophetic politics is more radical, more demanding
and probably more dangerous than royal politics (see 1 Sam
15:13–21).

Preacher and congregation will find this last surprising
turn in the narrative a difficult one. And no easy parallel
should be drawn. But it is a testimony to the simple-minded
prophetic conviction concerning the rule of Yahweh. Yahweh
makes no easy commitment to Israelite kings. They also
must face Yahweh's enigmatic sovereignty. From now on,
Ahab is under sentence. Just when he thought he had won
and had God in his pocket. And every power person who
seeks autonomous policy and power lives under sentence.
The prophetic legends are committed to a theocentric, if not
theocratic, politics. The king is left to wonder about what it
means that Yahweh is jealous.

A Story That Begins When It Should End
(21:1–29)

This is one of the best known and most powerful of all
these prophetic narratives. This text, like the entire cluster,
struggles with the relation of prophet and king, i.e., with the
question, what constitutes effective, faithful and legitimate
power?

(1) The narrative of vv. 1–16 is complete in and of itself.
It tells of two ways of power in conflict. It suggests two ways
of understanding land. On the one hand is *inheritance*, be-
longing intrinsically, traditionally and inalienably to a family or clan. On the other hand, land is *possession*, to be bought
and sold and traded. Thus the conflict is between a traditional tribalism and a new urban mercantilism.

(a) Naboth has the land. Ahab wants it. But he cannot
have it (vv. 1–4). The king may covet, but he proposes noth-

ing dishonest. The king abides by proper Israelite practice. The prophets had made him sullen in 20:43. That is not changed, but only increased. Ahab is sullen for not getting his way.

(b) The villain is not Ahab who is an innocent bystander in the narrative, but Queen Jezebel who knows none of the restraints which vex Ahab (vv. 5–14). What he cannot have, she knows how to secure for him. She proposes a quite different notion of kingship than is traditional in Israel. The narrative has already recognized that the marriage to Jezebel was Ahab's primal sin (1 Kings 16:31), for with the marriage came alien religion and disastrous social values (see 1 Kings 11:1–8). So she proposes to "give" to Ahab what is not hers to give (v. 7). Her ploy is to frame Naboth, have him executed as an enemy of the state. And when such a one is executed, the property inevitably falls to the crown (v. 14).

(c) The narrative should have ended in vv. 15–16. Everything is settled. Jezebel did what she had promised. There has been a complete inversion. Naboth who possessed is now dispossessed and dead. And the agent of inversion is this foreign queen who will have her way. She may understand political manipulation superbly, but she understands nothing of Israelite tradition.

(2) The story should have ended with v. 16. Everything is settled and complete. The inversion is symmetrical. But it does not end there. Where the story should have ended, is precisely where it begins. History begins in Israel when the prophet appears: "Then the word of the Lord came to Elijah..." (v. 17). A preachable point is that the story of our lives we imagine ended, and just then is when the word intrudes that begins it all afresh.

(a) In vv. 17–19, Elijah receives his orders. The speech of commissioning is in two predictable parts, the violation and the sentence. These three verses are structurally the center of the text. They completely redefine what Jezebel thought she was doing.

(b) The encounter of king and prophet is as dramatic as it is predictable. The king calls the prophet "enemy" (v. 20). And indeed, he is, for he is committed to dismantling the regime and declaring the king and queen illegitimate. In 18:17

Ahab called the prophet "troubler." But now things are even more intense. Now it is "enemy." And then follows (vv. 21–24) a devastating sentence for this supreme torah-breaker. There will be an end to this dynasty, the most solid regime the north had known. But against the torah of Yahweh, this regime is no more durable than that of Jeroboam (1 Kings 14:10–14) or that of Baasha (16:3–4). Kings come and go. And they go much sooner when they violate torah.

The general dismissal of the dynasty is stylized. This is followed by special reference to Jezebel (v. 23), for in this narrative, she is the quintessence of disobedience. Soon or late, God's rule will prevail. God will not be mocked, even by a Phoenician princess. This theologian wants to assert (one more time) that kings are not an important principle for history. They are bit-players on a stage where the principle actor and director is God's prophetic word. And so the word has its say and its way (see 2 Kings 9:36–37).

(3) The remainder of the narrative (vv. 25–29) presents a juxtaposition with which this historian must always live. And that is because history is simply like that.

(a) On the one hand, Ahab is the worst king (vv. 25–26). With a special credit to Jezebel, Ahab did enough to destroy Israel. He is a northern anticipation of the hopeless evil of Manasseh in the south (see 2 Kings 21). By any standard he should have perished on the spot.

(b) But on the other hand, Ahab does not perish as he should have (vv. 27–29). The theologian has this tight schedule for the death of the disobedient. But the historian must cope with the recalcitrant realities. As it happened, Ahab did not die promptly, for we have another narrative yet to come. The problem is that people do not behave and events do not fully happen according to any theory. The dynasty did not end abruptly as it should have. Ahab's two sons, Ahaziah and Jehoram, struggle their mediocre way for another eight years, until 842.

So the match of *theological urgency* and *historical realism* is reflected in these verses. Vv. 25–26 has no doubt of what is theologically appropriate. And vv. 27–29 does not hide the facts. The linkage between the two is accomplished by the repentance of Ahab (v. 27) which is what should have happened—even if it did not. The judgment is stayed for a time, but not cancelled. God's rule includes measured portions of judgment and grace. But we never know which is to be granted in any precise circumstance. So grace is given here for a time, even to this hopeless dynasty. But even that does not change the large picture of disobedience evoking a future of death.

The narrative action of this text permits a reflection on God's solidarity with the powerless against the powerful. It affirms the category of obedience in the realm of social relation as the stuff of faith, for disobedience to torah is how it is with Ahab and Jezebel. The shameless and unbridled use of royal power changes nothing about the resilient authority of the torah.

On the other hand, the latter portion of the text permits a more reflective approach to God's governance of history, to the incongruity between what should and what in fact does happen. And the narrative raises difficult issues of evil in God's world, or conversely, God's rule in an evil world. How in that world—that is, in this world—can one say, "God is ruler yet"? This is the question this theologian must ask and requires us to ask.

So there is the specificity of Naboth. But the narrative is not finally interested in Naboth. The real crisis concerns God's way in a world of destructive power against the powerless. And as in all these narratives, the break of God toward such demonic forces is the concrete prophetic word borne by a named person of faith. This theologian is relentless in making a connection between the largest theological claims and the most specific identification of concrete persons. But of course, it could hardly be otherwise in a faith on its way to incarnation.

"Truth" Disclosed Beyond Public Morality
(22:1–40)

The external history of Israel continues here from chapter 20, preoccupied with "the Syrian threat." This narrative is arranged so that there is an opening (vv. 1–6) and a closing (vv. 29–40), concerned with public history. Specifically the issue is the territory of Ramoth-Gilead, rich land between

Israel and Syria. It is rather like Alsace-Lorraine, a cause of endless conflict. But the middle body of the narrative (vv. 5–28) concerns the internal history and faith of Israel. And that crucial history consists in conflict between king and prophet, and eventually, between prophet and prophet. The issue turns on *"What is truth?"* (vv. 16, 22). It anticipates the same question by Pilate (John 18:38). In both narratives, here and in the Fourth Gospel, the truth is not known by the would-be rulers, but is offered by uncredentialed outsiders. And when the truth is asserted, it is such a strangeness (a scandal) that it is rejected as false. So a sermon might pose the question of truth: Who speaks it? How does one recognize it? What is "official truth" in our society? Who is offering alternative truth in our society, which is so strange (a scandal) that it is rejected as false?

(1) The narrative begins with war preparation (vv. 1–6). All war is about economics, even in the family, i.e., about land, territory, goods, power. The king of Israel (note how the narrative avoids hs name, for it does not want to grant him that legitimacy) wants land for which he has only a dubious claim. The king invites (forces?) his southern ally and counterpart to join his expansionism. Presumably Jehoshaphat is subservient and so he must go to war. But for this pious Judean king, war preparation includes guidance from the Lord (see 2 Kings 3:11–12). Thus the issue is joined. Ahab regards war (and kingship in general) as autonomous. He has learned well what Jezebel had to teach. By contrast Jehoshaphat sees war in reference to Yahweh. That is a first issue to explore, autonomous use of human power.

(2) In the center of that episode about war comes prophetic reality as something of an intrusion (vv. 7–28). The Judean king knows that prophets are to bear a transcendent message, underived from political circumstance. Prophetic faith is useless if it is only an echo of what the powerful already think is truth. Prophetic truth is expected to go beyond acceptable pragmatism. In the following series of engagements and exchanges, there are layers of duplicity, because "truth" is delicate and ambiguous. We are dealing with nothing less than God's will. And that will is not given in clear, transparent messages. It is always given in ways that tease

around our interests. The will of God is always yet to be clarified in struggle and dispute. If it is clear and easy, it likely contains large portions of wishful thinking.

(a) The *hired* prophets (see Jer 8:11; Micah 3:11) say what is expected. They offer easy assurances (vv. 10–12).

(b) The *summoned* prophet, the one who stands outside the conventional system of payoffs, also promises victory (vv. 13–15). His statement precisely echoes the hired voices. But the king is suspicious. Even though it is what he wants to hear, he knows better (v. 16). He does in fact know the difference between a *hired voice* that recites the party line, and a *summoned voice* which must tell against the party line. Coming from such an abrasive source, false assurances ring unmistakably false.

(c) In vv. 17–23, the narrative arrives at its center. After this opening deception, Micaiah gets to the real point. He has a word to speak that is discontinuous with royal reality. It comes from another source. The source is a glimpse into the heavenly throne room of God (see Isa 6:1–8; Jer 23:18, 22). Who can argue with such a credential? His message from the holy source is two-fold. First, there will be disaster—"no shepherd, no master." That is, the king will be killed (v. 17). Second, God so wants the death of Ahab that the false assurances of the false prophets are a ploy on the part of God to seduce Ahab into the death-trap of war (vv. 20–23). The lying prophets are not just "apple polishers" to the king, though they may intend to be. They speak what God has sent them to say, perhaps in spite of themselves. It is a divinely inspired lie in the service of truth. The truth is that the king who resists Yahweh must die. The lie is to entrap the king into an appropriate risk. This is an early and celebrated form of "entrapment."

Such a statement will not be easy to preach, for we have such "moral" notions of God. We find it unthinkable that God would use such a deceptive scheme. But the scheme must be seen in its largeness. The real issue is God's sovereignty. None can violate that, even in the service of lesser moral commitments.

(d) In vv. 24–28, we are given a bit of interplay between Micaiah, the "lying prophet," Zedekiah, and the king. Mi caiah is regarded as a traitor. And so he is imprisoned. But the die has been cast.

(3) The narrative now returns to the external history, the actual war (vv. 29–40).

(a) The battle is focused precisely on the person of the king (vv. 29–36). He is the real issue. Ahab is here presented as a coward. He forces the compliant Jehoshaphat to appear as Ahab while he himself seeks to hide as a common solider (v. 30). And at the same time, unbeknownst to Ahab, the Syrian enemy aims only to get Ahab. So the large political issue is intensely personalized. The Syrians seek only Ahab, while Ahab travels incognito.

But we are not dealing simply with rival kings. Perhaps they can deceive each other. But we are dealing here with God's intent, from which there is no hiding (see Ps 139:7–12). God is inescapable, even to this clever king. The truth of God will have its way. So the narrative (v. 34) attends to the inscrutable way of God. The king hides. An unnamed "certain man" sends an unknowing arrow.

And Ahab is struck! Surely it is an accident, a lucky hit, an unfortunate turn. Yes, unless one trusts God's word to have its say. In the last scene before his death (vv. 35–36), Ahab the coward functions heroically to lead his people, even though they are finally routed. But Ahab has it all wrong. He was *hero* to his people and *resistent* to God. No amount of heroism compensates for defiance of God's truth.

(b) The narrative adds its predictable judgment (vv. 37–40). It could not have happened otherwise. God's word had made promises against the king and the dynasty (1 Kings 21:21–24). Repentance had delayed the sentence (21:29). But nothing is in fact changed. Yahweh will be God.

The narrative is a complex one and there are many levels for a sermon. One might focus on the need for divine guidance in public affairs. Or the interplay between prophet and prophet. But the hard questions concern the interface of the inscrutable will of God and the haphazard way in which public events seem to happen. Thus in v. 38, the narrative is clear about why it all happened. But in v. 23, nothing is forced or insisted upon. It is all incidental. The narrative claims such incidental matters are in the service of God's truth. Even the lies of public policy serve the truth of God. Such an approach may bring us very close to the encounter of Jesus with Pilate (John 18:28—19:16). The lie of public policy required Jesus' death. But working in the midst of the entire scene was the irresistible purpose of God which in the end outlasted Pilate and the entire false order.

The question posed for the church is the governance of history, the rival claims of truth, and the irresistible poser of God's truth which surpasses human understanding.

An Odd Norm for Public Life (22:41–53)

This final paragraph of 1 Kings simply adds convention-al formulae to complete the chronology.

(1) Jehoshaphat is reckoned as one of the better kings in Judah (vv. 41–50). While he did not completely purify Judah (v. 43), he went far in a purge of false practice (v. 46). He is reported here to be a great warrior (v. 45) and his exploits (v. 48) are reminiscent of Solomon (see 1 Kings 10:11–12, 22). While Jehoshaphat was an effective and prosperous king, he also was mindful that finally kings are not autonomous and do not ultimately determine events in the public arena (see v. 5; 2 Kings 3:11; Prov 21:30–31).

(2) The note on Ahaziah (vv. 51–53) does not tell us much. But the reference to Baal in v. 53 prepares us for his death in 2 Kings 1, precisely because of his reliance on false gods (2 Kings 1:3, 6, 16).

The contrast between Jehoshaphat and Ahaziah is brief-ly but sharply drawn. The issue is always adherence to Yahweh and his torah. Jehoshaphat prospers in his reliance on Yahweh. Ahaziah turns elsewhere and pays dearly. It is an altogether simplistic notion of public faith. But it may be pertinent for asking very large questions about faith and public policy. In what does well-being consist (see Luke 19:42)?

Bibliography

Brueggemann, Walter, *Prophetic Imagination* (Philadelphia: Fortress Press, 1978).

Bryce, Glendon, *A Legacy of Wisdom* (Lewisburg: Bucknell University Press, 1979).

Buber, Martin, *The Prophetic Faith* (New York: Harper and Brothers, 1949).

Childs, Brevard, *Introduction to the Old Testament as Scripture* (Philadelphia: Fortress Press, 1979).

Childs, Brevard, *Isaiah and the Assyrian Crisis* (SBT 32; Naperville: Alec R. Allenson, Inc., 1967).

Ellul, Jacques, *The Politics of God and Politics of Man* (Grand Rapids: Eerdmans, 1972).

Maly, Eugene, *The World of David and Solomon* (Englewood: Prentice-Hall, 1966).

McCarthy, Dennis J., *Kings and Prophets* (Milwaukee: Bruce Publishing Co., 1968).

Mendenhall, George, "The Monarchy," *Interpretation* 29 (1975) 155–170.

Napier, B. Davie, *Word of God, Word of Earth* (Philadelphia: United Church Press, 1976).

Niebuhr, Reinhold, *Irony in American History* (New York: Scribner, 1952).

von Rad, Gerhard, *Studies in Deuteronomy* (SBT 9; Chicago: Henry Regnery Co., 1953).

Westermann, Claus, *Handbook to the Old Testament* (Minneapolis: Augsburg Publishing House, 1967).

Wolff, Hans Walter, "The Kerygma of the Deuteronomic Historical Work," in *The Vitality of Old Testament Traditions* by Walter Brueggemann and Hans Walter Wolff (Atlanta: John Knox Press, 1975) 83–100.